A SECRET REPORT TO
THE TRUE AMERICAN FAITH SOCIETY

Senior Citizens and Their Threat to America

by Hy Brett

A SECRET REPORT TO THE TRUE
AMERICAN FAITH SOCIETY by Hy Brett

Published by Brett Books in the United States of America

First Edition, 2014

For information email Brett Books at brettbooks@brettbooks.com.

Author services by Pedernales Publishing, LLC.
www.pedernalespublishing.com

Library of Congress Control Number: 2014940959

ISBN: 978-0-9899173-0-8 Paperback edition
ISBN: 978-0-9899173-1-5 Digital edition

Printed in the United States of America

Though a good deal is too strange to be believed,
nothing is too strange to have happened.

Thomas Hardy

INTRODUCTION BY THE AUTHOR

This book is a work of fiction, and bears no resemblance to any existing program for dealing with current problems. Back in 1729, when England was oppressing Ireland, Jonathan Swift, Dean of Saint Patrick's Cathedral in Dublin, was so appalled by the poverty in his homeland that he felt it his duty as a man of God to write *A Modest Proposal.* It was a satirical, over-the-top pamphlet in which he offered a possible though incredible solution to the problem: Why not turn the poor children of Ireland into food for rich Englishmen who might desire a change from their daily consumption at every meal of beef and pork, and of game, poultry and fish? Swift's pamphlet failed to move the hearts and minds of England's rulers, but many individuals did respond to it, and they began a campaign for change that finally resulted, after two hundred years of debate and bloodshed, in Irish independence.

In *A Secret Report to the True American Faith Society,* I aspire to applying Swift's method to what has been perceived as a problem of our own day—senior citizens and their threat to fiscal solvency. Disrespect to individuals, groups, organizations, races, religions and political parties is unintentional. Political, legal and religious quotations are true and accurate. I hope that my own modest proposal will be useful to the nation and lead to a bipartisan resolution of the problem. Maybe not immediately, but in fewer than two centuries. Anyhow, I will be content if it merely amuses and informs present-day readers.

Hy Brett
Brooklyn, NY

FOREWORD

Dear Harry:

On Sunday, September 1, I went down to Washington for a community tribute to a family friend who was retiring from the ministry. Afterward, on my way from his church to Union Station and then back to New York City and the fair borough of Brooklyn, a woman approached me on Massachusetts Avenue and pressed a small, square envelope into my hand.

It contained a computer disk, and I assumed that she represented one or another of the companies that offer new and improved access to the Internet, or so they claim. For a fleeting moment, I wondered why the woman, a senior citizen of at least seventy, was working so late on a Sunday, which is supposed to be a day of rest. But then I recalled that, with the high price of food, rent and other necessities, all too many of our seniors cannot live on their fixed incomes and must work part-time or even full-time.

"Thank you," I said to the woman. My friend's farewell sermon, based on Psalms 13:6, was devoted to the blessings that have been lavished upon us, and I smiled in gratitude for this new acquisition, nowhere mentioned in the Bible with the possible exception of Matthew 13:47: "Again, the kingdom of heaven is like unto a net, that was cast into the sea, and gathered of every kind."

"You're welcome, sir. Be prepared for an eye-opener."

Naturally, in my total ignorance of how both public- and private-sector leaks are perpetrated in the Beltway, I thought she was referring to enhanced surfing, or to entry, for a monthly surcharge, to the hitherto secret chat rooms of the sort of financial wizards who, according to a report in *The New York Times,* are privy to the tax laws that "currently grant certain favors only to the very wealthiest."

A few weeks later, back home in Brooklyn, a disastrous download of pictures of Fluffy, my granddaughter's new cat, convinced me that the time had finally come to upgrade my portal to the Internet. My bright, new disk from Washington bore an interlocking S, R and D within a circle of thirteen stars, and when I inserted it into my CD-ROM drive, I soon saw something very unexpected on my screen, something that was, indeed, an eye-opener. My first thought was that a worm or virus called maybe Murder USA had infected my computer. But then it dawned on me that the woman on Massachusetts Avenue might have been emulating the brave citizens who had blown the whistle on Enron, WorldCom and the intelligence community, and that she now sought to expose another great threat to the country.

I had no reason to doubt that her heart was in the right place, and that she wished only to prevent what she perceived to be a wrong that might one day, and sooner rather than later, be perpetrated against at least forty million Americans. But as I read the often incredible contents of her disk, I told myself to be objective, and to give a fair hearing to what, in our current moral, commercial and political climates, was surely a perfectly legal if novel solution to what pundits across the political spectrum have identified as a national crisis. One of these experts, the most senior fellow at a prestigious think tank, considers the problem to be even more dangerous to America than abortion or gun control, and has suggested that it was high time for the president "to press the panic button," obviously a euphemism for the taking of strong measures, perhaps the very measures discussed on my new disk.

After reading and rereading the disk, I think that my wisest move is to pass it on to you, Harry, a guy who has served four administrations, both Republican and Democratic. You have my okay to destroy it. Or to disseminate its contents in full or in part. Whatever you do, I know it will be the best course for the country that we love and wish to preserve for the true benefit of all its citizens.

With best wishes,
Greg

A SECRET REPORT TO
THE TRUE AMERICAN FAITH SOCIETY

Concerning

SENIOR CITIZENS AND THEIR THREAT
TO AMERICA

Prepared by

SENECA RESEARCH & DEVELOPMENT
ASSOCIATES

SENECA RESEARCH & DEVELOPMENT
ASSOCIATES

Founded in 1903

*"Idealism without realism is impotent. Realism
without idealism is immoral."*
Richard M. Nixon

OMNIA VINCIT VERITAS

Chairpersons	*Rosemary Canfield, Ph.D.*
	Victor J. Shawn, D.D., M.B.
Chairman Emeritus	*Frederick Peabody, M.B.A.*
Executive Director	*Sanford B. Estes*
Director of Studies	*Gloria Monke*
Director of Administration	*Cushing "Smoky" Bayberry III*
Senior Policy Coordinator	*Trevor Ashley, J.D.*
Director for Research	*Melvin Diamond, Ph.D.*

Hy Brett

Geriatric Studies Coordinator	*Avery F. Sawyer, M.D., Ph.D.*
Media Coordinator	*Heather Ehrling, Ph.D.*
Legal Advisor	*Martha E. Scourby, J.D., Ph.D.*
Financial Consultant	*Peter Nettleton, M.B.A.*
Washington Consultant	*Sherry Straw, M.A.*
Chief Information Officer	*Anita Queen, Ph.D.*
Rhetoric Consultant	*Kevin Bowers, Ph.D.*

DEDICATED TO

John Jay (1745-1829) A Founding Father and first Chief Justice of the Supreme Court. In the 2nd of *The Federalist Papers*, the series of articles that urged the ratification of the Constitution, he wrote the following: "Nothing is more certain than the indispensable necessity of government; and it is equally undeniable that whenever and however it is instituted, the people must cede to it some of their natural rights, in order to vest it with requisite powers."

The above is the sort of pragmatic wisdom that prompted President George Washington to propose John Jay as the nation's first chief justice of the Supreme Court. Both of these great Americans would have agreed wholeheartedly with Roman poet Virgil that "The noblest motive is the public good."

TO THE HONORABLE OFFICERS OF
THE TRUE AMERICAN FAITH SOCIETY

Thank you for inviting Seneca Research and Development to participate in the discussion of senior proliferation, which we and other impartial groups have identified as the greatest immediate threat to America in the decades ahead. We consider it an even greater threat than high taxes and big government. Than narcotics, global warming and the decline of deference to religious and secular authority. Than widespread criticism of the wise and just decisions of the U.S. Supreme Court.

Increasingly, to our dismay, the Court is perceived by even average citizens to be what the Founding Fathers had always intended it to be but never publicized, namely, a crypto-political rather than a purely legal institution, a sanctification, so to speak, of the interests of property owners and of other dominant groups and classes. On June 18, 1787, during a convention gathered to debate a Federal Constitution, Alexander Hamilton, chief of staff to General George Washington, articulated the philosophy of most of his colleagues at the State House in Philadelphia: "All communities divide themselves into the few and the many. The first are the rich and wellborn, the others are the mass of the people…. The people are turbulent and changing; they seldom judge and determine right. Give therefore to the first class a distinct, permanent share in the government…."

Your society can rest assured that once the problem of senior proliferation has been resolved to your satisfaction, we would be delighted to offer you our thoughts on all those other problems, both domestic and foreign, that vex all true Americans who are dedicated to our traditions of faith and justice.

We know well that, like former presidents Lyndon Johnson and Ronald Reagan, the officers of your society prefer to think and act by gut feelings of patriotism and religious instinct, and that your time to read reports and proposals is limited. Nevertheless, we feel that this report, though perhaps lengthy and detailed, will not be a total waste of your valuable time, and we would first like to focus your attention by a brief reminder of just a few of our efforts on behalf of past and recent clients. For good and sufficient reason, they prefer to remain anonymous at this time, *and perhaps even for all time* (italics suggested by Derek Strudel, Jr., managing partner of the Washington-based law firm of Franklin Duval Strudel, LLP):

- Arranging for federal and state banking agencies to approve of the de facto elimination of interest on savings accounts. Since our intervention in 2009, banks have flourished as never before, and the salaries and bonuses of officers are at an all-time high.

- The placement of Monica Lewinsky in the White House where she would arouse the lust of President Bill Clinton. That Mr. Clinton was not later impeached and removed from office was not our fault but that of congressional leaders who failed to "run with the ball," possibly because they feared exposure of their own, even worse sexual misconduct.

- The creation and orchestration of the financial crisis that caused voters in 2010 to elect a sufficiency of Republicans to control the House of Representatives and nullify the left-wing agendas of President Obama and of the Democratic majority in the Senate.

- The creation and orchestration of the movement that questioned and will forever continue to question the birthplace and citizenship of President Obama. Should he have the audacity to attempt to remain in government after his disservice in the White House, we will go on to question the legitimacy of his marriage to the former Michelle LaVaughn Robinson, and then encourage Donald Trump and other cooperating sources of information, especially Fox News and Rush Limbaugh, to suggest (1) the existence of mistresses past and present, and (2) of other wives not only in Chicago but also in Brooklyn, Hawaii, Kenya and Singapore, and (3) intercourse with expensive prostitutes at luxurious hotels, among them the Cartegena in Colombia and the Mayflower in Washington.

- The creation, launching and funding of the Tea Party, and the transformation of such gifted women as Sarah Palin and Michelle Bachmann from relative obscurity to leaders uniquely fit for the presidency in these perilous times both at home and abroad.

- The costume "malfunction" that resulted in the exposure of Janet Jackson's breast at the 2004 Super Bowl. Though of brief duration and not totally revealing of the aforementioned breast, the exposure stirred up a moral and religious tempest that lasted throughout the election season and is still gaining momentum. During a future election season we hope to repeat our coup de théâtre with a more voluptuous young woman, perhaps a past or present Miss Georgia, the Peach State. Meanwhile, a focus group will be testing the electoral effect of revealing not a single but both breasts.

- The ongoing training and placement of White House correspondents whom we program to ask "softball" questions of presidents favored by clients and hard "spitball" questions of objectionable presidents.

- The training of pundits with appeal to the lesser educated, and then their placement in the media and appropriate think tanks, whether existent or newly created.
- The creation of the following generic, all-purpose sound bite for clients who, despite the usually effective precautions by lawyers and public relations experts, may unexpectedly be confronted with a hard question by an unfriendly reporter: "I make policy decisions based on what is best for America and for the creation of jobs for my fellow Americans. These decisions have nothing at all to do with politics. People who suggest otherwise are ill-informed, and [crescendo] are themselves motivated by politics. God Bless America!"

MISSION STATEMENT

Words are a goodly part of our stock in trade, and yet we cannot find the ones that will fully express our gratitude for this opportunity to activate yet once again the philosophy that ever since 1903 has inspired our motto: "In considerations of public policy, the interests of our nation, the greatest that has ever existed on earth, must always come first."

Seneca Research and Development Associates is, of course, named for Lucius Annaeus Seneca (7 B.C.— 65 A.D), the Roman statesman-philosopher. He, like his father, the rhetorician Marcus Annaeus Seneca (54 B.C.?—39 A.D.), believed that a short life with honor is preferable to a long life with shame and dependency. True, Seneca the Younger did not self-terminate until, suspected of participation in the Piso conspiracy, he was ordered to do so by the Emperor Nero, but that should in no way detract from his glory and reputation for wisdom and public service. In 1998-99, the impeachment proceedings revealed, eventually, the presence in Congress of Republican leaders who, like the perfidious President Clinton, had not lived up to their professed standards of morality, especially in marital relationships. And yet, according to Dr. Maurice Shield, author of *Congress, Contingency and Morality*, the mere recommendation of those high standards to the American people was, platonically speaking, an absolute and autonomous act of virtue in itself, and surely preferable to a recommendation for immorality. Dr. Shield observed in an obiter dictum, "As they say in divinity schools, if you can't practice what you preach, then the next best thing is to preach as if Jesus were standing over your shoulder."

Contents

AN AMERICAN AGENDA FOR THE AGED

Currently, no domestic problem is more critical and demanding of wisdom, compassion and a sound post-neoconservative philosophy than the one addressed in this report, which recommends the immediate implementation of a Senior Citizen Growth and Opportunity Act. Such legislation, and its endorsement and wide dissemination by the media, think tanks and custom-designed grass roots organizations will surely result in a nexus of budget-sensitive and yet high-yield programs for senior maintenance in the decades ahead. And perhaps even until the end of the century.

Ever since 1935, Social Security has provided retirement benefits for tens of millions of Americans. Four generations of Americans have relied on a bloated, inefficient government to keep the alleged promises it made to them during their working years. As demographics change and costs increase, the great challenge we face is to make sure that the Social Security system and other entitlement programs are adjusted for the true, long-range benefit of the country and not for the ever-increasing expectations of a population exposed for decades to leftist demagogues and their socio-cultural misrepresentations. Our plan to update and eventually eliminate the afore-mentioned programs include:

- Transfer of all retirement funds from the Social Security Administration to the private sector and to a corporation supervised by a newly created National Association of Bankers and Stock Brokers.
- The abolition of Obamacare, and the promotion of a philosophy of Freedom of Choice regarding medical care for both seniors and pre-seniors. And then, the orchestration of the aforementioned Freedom of Choice into the eventual total replacement of Medicaid and Medicare by medical facilities owned and operated by the private sector.
- An increase in economic growth that is not dependent upon an outmoded and unrealistic preference for maximum employment of lower and middle-class Americans. They must be conditioned to understand that investors and international bankers, money managers and hedge fund managers are now the prime movers in both in the manufacturing and service sectors of the economy. Therefore, in the spirit of *Citizens United v. Federal Election Commission, McCutcheon v. Federal Election Commission* and

other recent rulings by our good friends on the Supreme Court, the constitutionally protected interests of our de facto leaders must include the highest possible financial incentives for themselves and both assured and ever-increasing profits for their companies.

Inspired by the work of such outstanding organizations as the American Bankers Association and the National Rifle Association, which have served and protected the country since 1875 and 1871 respectively, we, like you, consider it our patriotic duty to help rescue the country from the stranglehold of the socialist policies that have led to the present federal deficit, imbalance of trade, financial crisis, chaos abroad and the threat of terrorism at home. The time has now arrived for the giant steps we recommend in this report. And they must be taken at once, while the window of opportunity is still wide open, thanks to the control of the House of Representatives by the political party that is and always will be totally dedicated to fiscal responsibility. Paraphrasing the words of President George Washington in his First Annual Message to Congress on January 8, 1790, "To be prepared for war against entitlement programs is one of the most effective means of preserving domestic peace and harmony."

Without access to doctors and medicine, and sustained mostly by prayer and rum, Washington and his gallant troops survived the bitter winter of 1777 at Valley

Forge, and they then went on to defeat the British and their ruthless mercenaries from other countries. Were he with us now, Washington would be especially disturbed about Medicare Part D with its enrollment of millions of seniors and disabled people, and the absence of prayer and rum in an appendix to its formulary of prescription drugs.

We are drawing close to our D-Day, the day of deliverance from a menace that has been threatening our beloved country ever since the enactment of Social Security in 1935 and then of Medicaid and Medicare in 1964. Needless to say, all three programs were inflicted upon us by Democratic administrations, and they were opposed tooth and nail by the great majority of Republicans in government and in the private sector. The warning of President Herbert Hoover is as relevant now as it was in 1930, when, in the early days of the Great Depression, he foresaw the inevitable results of crypto-socialist economics: "Prosperity cannot be restored by raids on the public treasury." President Hoover, son of a hard-working Quaker blacksmith, was born in 1874, a golden era when the pioneer spirit of Daniel Boone and Davy Crockett still prevailed in the land, and when the provision of government relief was justified only in cases of great natural disaster and imminent starvation.

Throughout human history, and most definitely during our own Colonial period, the time frame that inspired the Declaration of Independence and the Constitution, both faith-based and secular belief systems have beseeched people to assist one another through interpersonal acts of kindness and not through government, and very definitely not through business enterprises whose sacred mission it is to provide (1) salaries, bonuses, stock options and pensions for executives and directors, (2) profits for owners and investors, (3) campaign contributions to political candidates in good standing with the U.S. Chamber of Commerce and National Rifle Association, (4) goods and services for customers who pay their bills, and (5) engage lawyers and bill collectors to interact with customers who do not pay for duly contracted goods and services. Matthew 22:39 adjures us to "love thy neighbor as thyself." What else is this but a call for individual initiatives, either alone or through family networks or through faith-based and secular charities such as The Salvation Army and The United Way? Because they substitute long-term government aid for the individual, biblically sanctioned initiatives that have led to our greatness, the four major entitlement programs—Social Security, Medicaid, Medicare and Medicare Part 4 Prescription Plans—were wrong when they began and they are even more wrong in this second decade of the new millennium, when the country is unprepared to satisfy the entitlements that, nowhere mentioned in the Constitution, are expected by the post-World War II generation, commonly called the baby boomers. According to the nonpartisan Congressional Research Service, more than 12 million

Americans already rely on government for such long-term care services as nursing homes and home health aides.

And according to the Census Bureau, the 76 million future occupants of the safety net will enjoy even more than the current life expectancy of 80.8 years for women and 75.6 years for men. And the number who will reach the age of 100 increases every year by more than 7 percent. By the year 2050, we will have ten times the number of centenarians we have today. And because of the exposure of baby boomers to public radio, public television and suchlike popular culture during their formative years, ethno-demographers believe that all too many of them lack true public spirit and any appreciation of self-sacrifice, the sort of self-sacrifice that motivates current leaders of the three branches of our government to serve the country for a fraction of the remuneration they would have received in the private sector as lawyers and lobbyists, bankers and brokers, business executives and motivation speakers, senior and even junior fellows of think tanks sponsored by billionaires who want everyone to become as rich as they are.

We are compelled by the longevity revolution to reconsider all the stages of life and their implication for the economy. In the course of our preparation of this report, a principal guide was the spirit of the late Reverend Jerry Falwell, who wrote in one of his many masterpieces, *Strength for the Journey*, that "Life is a journey.... We who call ourselves Christians believe that the journey begins and ends with God. He created us at the beginning of life and He will welcome us home when this life is over."

Premature disclosure of our contemplated plans for the nation in general and for our beloved seniors in particular, which include a total restructuring and eventual elimination of all governmental entitlement programs, will almost certainly lead to their distortion, dilution and defeat in the marketplace of ideas, which, like in any other marketplace, whether of baked beans or Chanel coats costing $9000, must first be primed with advertising and public relations campaigns for maximum acceptance of the product. In a worst-case scenario, premature disclosure and the resultant malicious criticism by, among others, supporters of Occupy Wall Street and related alien ideologies, would lead to an undesirable change in the unique political system that, in the words of President Dwight D. Eisenhower, who led our worldwide crusade for democracy in World War II, has brought us "human dignity, economic freedom, individual responsibility...and has given to our people the highest standard of living that the world has ever known and has made of this nation a force for justice and peace."

To sum up, unless we stop this creeping socialism in its tracks and return to the cost-conscious socioeconomic policies of our glorious past, our creditors will soon start charging us the high interest rates they already charge such improvident countries as Greece, Ireland and Portugal. Otherwise, we will be bankrupted within a decade by the

78 million baby boomers as they retire and demand their Medicare and Social Security benefits.

We are confident that once they become the law of the land and are actualized by command-and-control specialists from relevant federal agencies, our guidelines will become a template for more effective policies in such other problem areas as (1) public assistance for the unemployed and unemployable, (2) affirmative action programs for minorities, (3) special facilities for the handicapped, (4) the alleged constitutional rights of gays, and of women to make their own decisions regarding abortion and childbearing instead of respecting the democratic process and deferring to the authority of the state and authorized religious leaders.

Finally, at this point, we wish to thank the anonymous philanthropist who has funded this and related studies since 1994, when one of his idols, then House Speaker Newt Gingrich, activated a "Republican Revolution" and a Contract with America that called for tax cuts, smaller government, and an end to the political corruption and social decay that had become the hallmark of the Clinton administration. Our patron now prefers anonymity, but in time to come his countrymen will surely know of his generosity, and be as grateful to him as they currently are to other individuals and families—Carnegie, Ford, Gates, Koch, Mellon, Rockefeller—who have lent their illustrious names to great foundations. We offer our assurance to The True American Faith Society that, once enacted, our program for seniors will require no additional expenditure, tax increases, or manipulation of public funds.

On the contrary, the Senior Citizen Growth and Opportunity Act will be structured to take full advantage of the Society's well-known desire for maximum privatization and outsourcing of government functions, including domestic security and military operations in Iraq, Afghanistan and all other present and future overt and covert venues for the creation and maintenance of freedom and democracy. Government at all levels will outsource contracts for the execution of senior services to corporations that, like any other private-sector producer of a good or service, will be formed with the aid of an investment bank, will be listed on an appropriate stock exchange, and will have an initial public offering after the usual paid notices and the engagement of a celebrity spokesperson of the stature of former New York City Mayor Rudy Giuliani or of master builder Donald Trump. A proven fighter for traditional values, he/she will interact with the media and attend such photo opportunities as prayer meetings and state fairs, barbeques and ball games. The delivery of public services by the private sector is well established, and according to a *New York Times* article by Harvard professor Stephen Goldsmith and William D. Eggers, director at Deloitte Research and a fellow at the Manhattan Institute, "the Federal government now spends $100 billion more annually for outside contracts than it does on employee's salaries." For an optimum implementation of the program, the ever-increasing preference for franchising may well be "the way to go," in which case we will certainly consult the experts at such successful enterprises as McDonald's, Pizza Hut and Mary Kay.

At the same time, we hasten to agree with leaders in Washington and the private sector that the free market system, like any other fine mechanism, needs a lubricant from time to time, and that it works with maximum efficiency when a very few key industries receive government subsidies, tariff protection, tax rebates and other benefits. Among our approved recipients of state and federal funds are, and should continue to be, faith-based schools and charities, pig farms and cattle raising and fishing, mining, aviation, shipping, trucking and rail transportation, health care and pharmaceutical research, radio and television, banking, insurance, telecommunications, munitions, agriculture, lumber, oil and natural gas, publishing, the construction and maintenance of sports stadiums and of highways leading to golf courses and country clubs. These incentives, which reduce tax revenues by only a trifle over $300 billion a year, are a small price to pay for the continuation of free enterprise and the American Way of Life. "You don't make the poor richer by making the rich poor." This truism was said by the late British Prime Minister Winston Churchill, whose mother came from Brooklyn, the Borough of Churches, and who made it a point to daily place him on her knee and teach him

American as well as religious values. This fact of life is well understood and practiced along our corridors of power, especially at the United States Supreme Court, where devotion to the precepts of the Founding Fathers and a strict adherence to the Constitution usually compels a majority of justices to favor business over people.

We acknowledge that "Senior Citizen Growth and Opportunity Act" may be a somewhat awkward name for our proposed legislation, which would usher in a new birth of freedom for our seniors, enabling them to exercise additional rights and powers, and to shed inhibitions that have stunted their spiritual growth. Should our program win the endorsement of The True American Faith Society and its nationwide network of fundraisers, we will make every effort to engage the services of communications genius Dr. Frank Luntz, author of the bestseller *Words That Work*. To cite only a single example of his verbal virtuosity, by referring to the inheritance tax as the "death tax," he has been able to change the hearts and minds of citizens and incite them to clamor for the elimination of an odious outrage against all economic classes, but especially the poor and middle-class people. To assure their continued faith in a free market economy with its frequent depressions, recessions and longtime unemployment, the poor and middle class must be conditioned to believe that if they work hard all their lives at one or more jobs, and finally achieve their birthright as Americans and become millionaires if not billionaires, their assets would one day go to their loved ones and not be appropriated and misspent on entitlements by the federal government and its bureaucrats. We are hopeful that, if he agrees with our vision and comes aboard, Mr. Luntz will be no less successful in the popularization of our own program.

The subject of public acceptance of a new program or product always, and with good reason, evokes the name and achievements of Clotaire Rafaille, the psychiatrist and medical anthropologist who, according to *The New York Times*, "is paid top dollar by American corporations to tell them what consumers want from their coffee, toilet paper, artificial sweetener, luggage, cheese and political candidates...." The Society may rest assured that once it gives the green light to The Senior Citizen Growth and Opportunity Act, or whatever other maxi-motivational name is suggested by Dr. Frank Luntz and his focus groups and polling scientists, every effort will be made to secure also the unique services of Dr. Rafaille.

A FEW TIMELY THOUGHTS ABOUT
LIFE CYCLES

To die well is to die willingly.
Seneca

To every thing there is a season, and a time to every purpose under the heaven: A time to be born, and a time to die; a time to plant, and a time to pluck up that which is planted.

Ecclesiastes 3:1-2

There is a time for ripeness for death...when it is reasonable we should drop and make room for another growth. When we have lived our generation out, we should not wish to encroach on another.

Thomas Jefferson

We can no longer treat life as something that has trickled down to us. We have to deal with it deliberately, devise its social organization, alter its tools, formulate its method, educate and control it.

Walter Lippmann
Drift and Mastery

Right action follows right purpose. We may not at all times be able to divine the future, but if our aims are high and unselfish, somehow and in some way the right end will be reached.

President William McKinley

We've got a duty to die and get out of the way with all of our machines and artificial hearts and everything else like that and let the other society, our kids, build a reasonable life.

**Former Colorado Governor
Richard D. Lamm**

THE PROBLEM

There is a tide in the affairs of men,
Which, taken at the flood, leads on to fortune;
Omitted, all the voyage of their life
Is bound in shallows and miseries.
Shakespeare

Early in the first millennium, Lucius Annaeus Seneca, the Roman statesman and philosopher, said, "*Non est ad astra mollis e terris via.*" There is no easy way from the earth to the stars. And this ancient wisdom remains just as true in America today. We know that we must take certain steps in order to survive and prosper as a nation, and to fulfill our divine mission, by force if necessary, of bringing democracy and freedom and an Electoral College, and low taxes and a free market system to all the world, from the mountains of Afghanistan to the barbed wire fences of North Korea. But we are stuck in place by precepts and practices that have outlived their usefulness.

Surely the time has come to heed the pronouncement of Dr. Henry Kissinger in a previous time of national distress: "In crises, the most daring course is often safest."

Regarding senior proliferation and its effects, Dr. Kissinger might well say now what he said in 1973 about the U.S. endorsed coup d'etat against Salvador Allende, the democratically elected president of Chile: "I don't see why we need to stand by and watch a country go communist due to the irresponsibility of its people. The issues are much too important for the Chilean voters to be left to decide for themselves."

Statements of reality about our aging population are never pleasant to hear, but they must be heeded and dealt with. And the good news is that, inspired by the policies of current and former presidents in the fields of education and the environment, we and our world-class experts have developed a both compassionate and cost-effective way of dealing with the problem, which was growing at an alarming rate long before the catastrophe of 9/11 and the resultant expenditures upon security at home and military operations abroad.

According to double-blind research conducted by Avery F. Sawyer, our coordinator of geriatric studies, it is a certainty that with proper conditioning of our citizens, participation in the program recommended in this report, namely, the reduction and prevention of superfluous geriatrics, will one day be regarded as much a public responsibility as jury duty, military service, and the paying of taxes unless, of course, they can be legally avoided with the aid of lobbyists and lawyers and accountants, friends in government, or by moving a corporation's legal domicile from stateside to a post-office box or lawyer's cubicle in the Cayman Islands. FYI, one of the Cayman's many other attractions is a 23-acre marine park that is devoted especially to the care of sea turtles.

Medical science now treats aggressively the multitude of physical and even mental ailments that were once considered inevitable companions of advanced nonreversible hypometabolism, which is better known to laypersons as the aging process. There are currently 36.7 million Americans of 65 and over who are entitled to Medicare and the full benefits of Social Security. (This figure excludes 5.3 million disabled pre-seniors who receive similar benefits.) They constitute 13 percent of the population, and their number is projected to double over the next three decades to nearly 70 million, or fully 20 percent of the population. The Census Bureau projects the 65-plus population to be 53.2 million in 2020, 69.4 million in 2030, and 80 million in 2050. This projection does not include the astronomic gross cost of the Medicare Part D prescription benefits, estimated as high as $2 trillion for its first decade, that presidents and members of Congress had often used as an election "gimmick" for many years and that finally, for their own political health, they had to provide to seniors preparatory to the touch-and-go election season of 2004. But let us take heart in these words of the late Judge Robert H. Bork: "[Law is] vulnerable to the winds of intellectual or moral fashion, which it then validates as the commands of our most basic concept."

Assuredly, the startling expenditures to be incurred by Medicare in the near future, as mentioned above, will be increased exponentially within the decade by the genome-based research that gerontologists predict will ameliorate if not totally eliminate many current afflictions of the aged and further increase their life expectancy, which according to the latest figures from the U.S Census Bureau, as already brought to your attention, are 80.8 years for women and 75.6 years for men. (As yet, the Census Bureau does not classify the life expectancy of transsexuals, either males into females or vice versa.)

The subject of this report would have come as no surprise to the Reverend Thomas Robert Malthus (1766-1834), the British economist who in *An Essay on the Principle of Population* (1798) shocked his countrymen with a frank discussion of population, the causes of overpopulation, and of whether it was really the responsibility of government rather than of individuals to take preventive and corrective measures when Nature alone fails to provide a sufficiency of food, land, and other resources. It is quite likely that, were he alive, the Reverend Malthus would be most sympathetic to our Going Ahead program for seniors. Certainly, judging by the exhortations in his landmark study, the Reverend Malthus would disapprove of, and devote many a Sunday sermon to, the spiritual dangers of such a modern-day government program as, for example, Aid to Dependent Children. With all the eloquence he had displayed in sermons and lectures at, appropriately, Jesus

College, the heart and soul of Cambridge University, he would implore parents of dependent children to desist in their nocturnal frolics, and in that way help sustain their current offspring.

According to the latest figures from the Census Bureau, public pensions absorb 7.2 percent of the gross domestic product in the United States. And thanks to the benefits of government-sponsored long-term care, the 2010 Census has estimated there to be 70,490 centenarians in the country, and the figure may increase tenfold by 2050. Unless we quickly institute a situation-specific counteraction such as the Senior Citizen Growth and Opportunity Act, our public pensions will, as they already do in Italy, be absorbing fully 15 percent of the gross domestic product. Sad to say, the Mediterranean Diet with its red wine and olive oil is not only life prolonging but also fiscally depleting, as the finance ministers of Spain, Greece and Italy have already learned. (In a spirit of pro bono, our subsidiaries in the aforementioned three countries are suggesting, as a counter-measure toward financial stability, that the nutritional value of a 45° slice of pizza be raised to at least 620 calories, total fat to 9 grams of which 3 grams are saturated fat, cholesterol to 16mg, sodium to 455mg, and total carbohydrates to at least 30g.)

Whether they be a fetus in the womb or tottering to the tomb, all American citizens most certainly have a right to life, but not, in a time of federal, state and municipal budget deficits, to so long a life that their Social Security and Medicare benefits become a burden and threat to the nation. May the Good Lord and their fellow Americans bless the seniors who have lived to partake with overflowing cups of their increasingly costly benefits, but after a prolonged period of enjoying the fruits of the earth, it behooves them to become fact-sensitive and to unburden their juniors. Toward that noble and civic-minded end, our seniors must be exposed to a daily mix of conscience-raising messages that will increase their sense of responsibility to the nation. The messages must and will be presented in the simplest and most emotional words, the same words with which the aforementioned Dr. Clotaire Rafaille and his colleagues on Madison Avenue sell their beer and perfume, and with which Dr. Frank Luntz wins the election of clients to the executive and legislative branches of government and through those two branches determine the selection of a Supreme Court that, though decked in black robes and not crowns of gold, has more unquestioned power than many a monarch of old, including, for example, King Louis XIV of France (1638-1715), who said: "It is legal because I wish it so." King Louis XIV usually preferred to conduct his affairs of state in bed, but in his otherwise comprehensive memoirs, Louis de Rouvroy, duc de Saint-Simon, does not name the mistress who shared the king's bed when he delivered the above remark. This legal philosophy, we are sure, would never occur to American judges and justices of both political parties.

SOME INSPIRATION FOR THE TASK BEFORE US

In thy light shall we see light.
Psalms 36:9

We deeply appreciate the guidance of Professor Avery F. Sawyer, our Senior Coordinator of Geriatric Studies, in the selection of the following quotations. Culled from the sacred and secular wisdom of all ages and all lands, the quotations are intended to remove any lingering doubts that the Senior Citizen Growth and Opportunity Act is on the right track, morally speaking. Professor Sawyer was a co-founder of the North American Association of Board-Certified Bioethicists, and is also the author of *Alternatives to the Decline and Fall of the United States: Toward a Broader Perception of Demographic Trends*. He is a frequent guest on cable television, and as a public speaker is represented by the same bureau as former First Ladies Hillary Clinton and Laura Bush. In addition, he manages a Little League baseball team in his hometown of Hampton Falls, Maryland, and is a former vice president of the Empire State Association for Public Opinion Research and Development. At the age of forty-four, Professor Sawyer has attained the courage, tolerance, and mellow wisdom that we would usually expect to find only in a man of twice his years. We believe that his relative youth allows him to address objectively and without fear or favor the problems of the elderly, and we have tentatively adopted his suggestion that seniors who take advantage of the program should be called either Senior Samaritans or Golden Oldies, depending upon context and occasion.

Professor Sawyer looks forward not only to his team's once again winning a Little League pennant after a lapse of forty years but also to being of an age to join the ranks of our Senior Samaritans. His great regret is that his parents, the Reverend D. Philip Sawyer and Rochelle Marie Sawyer, died before the inception of the Going Ahead program, which would have enabled them, like their lifelong role model, Revolutionary War hero Nathan Hale, to give up their lives for their country. Not a day passes that Professor Sawyer does not think of their breakfast-nook sampler with the words of Harriet Beecher Stowe: "Half the misery in the world comes from want of courage to speak and to hear the truth plainly, and in a spirit of love."

I think of death as some delightful journey
That I shall take when all my tasks are done.
                                    Ella Wheeler Wilcox

Not lost, but gone before.
                                    Horace

To everything there is a season, and a time to every purpose under the heaven. A time to be born, and a time to die; a time to plant, and a time to pluck up that which is planted.
Ecclesiastes 3:1-2

It is not possible to fight beyond your strength, even if you strive.
Homer, *The Iliad,*
Book XIII, l.787

Until he is dead, do not call a man happy, but only lucky.
Herodotus I, 32

There is no medicine to be found for a life which is fled.
Ibycus

Death is the supreme festival on the road to freedom
Dietrich Bonhoeffer,
Letters and Papers on the Road to Freedom

Death. An instantaneous state, without past or future. Indispensable for entering eternity.
Simone Weill, *Gravity and Grace*

Think not disdainfully of death, but look on it with favor; for death is one of the things that Nature wills.
Marcus Aurelius, *Meditations*

Yea, though I walk through the valley of the shadow of death, I will fear no evil; for thou art with me; thy rod and thy staff they comfort me.

Psalms 23:4

O death, where is thy sting? O grave, where is thy victory?
1 Corinthians 15:55

One short sleep past, we wake eternally,
And death shall be no more; death, thou shalt die.
John Donne, *Holy Sonnets*

Death is the liberator of him whom freedom cannot release, the physician of him whom medicine cannot cure, and the comforter of him whom time cannot console.
Charles Caleb Colton, *Lacon*

Mad from life's history,
Glad to death's mystery,
Swift to be hurl'd -
Anywhere, anywhere,
Out of the world!

Thomas Hood,
"Bridge of Sighs"

What seem to us but dim funereal tapers, may be heaven's distant lamps.
Longfellow

We go to the grave of a friend, saying, "A man is dead," but angels throng around him, saying, "A man is born."
Henry Ward Beecher

TOWARD A SOLUTION

*Death is sometimes a punishment, often a gift,
and to many a favor.*
Seneca

Regrettably, whether they be Republicans or Democrats, our public servants in charge of senior maintenance have not been paying proper attention to the profound lessons of the life cycles of Nature. What is needed, and as soon as possible, is a whole new philosophy, a whole new attitude about the true nature of the seniors and the super-seniors in our midst. In a rapidly changing world and environment, can we still allow our seniors to be perceived as fountainheads of wisdom and stability? Are they really the benign and lovable figures that are so often depicted in film and folklore, in books and plays?

Social forces constantly make, interpret, reinterpret, and unmake laws, all of which activity is defined by legal scholar Lon Fuller as "the enterprise of subjecting human conduct to the governance of rules." Social forces are also responsible for the concepts we call "morality" and for the practices we attribute to "human nature." Let us not forget, although it may be a comfort to do so, that our Founding Fathers approved of slavery and believed not only that all men, if white, are created equal but also that all women, white as well as Negro and Indian, could not be endowed with the political, legal, educational, and vocational rights that were so essential for the life, liberty, and pursuit of happiness of the aforementioned white men. However vile his character or abysmal his intelligence, a young white man could vote and run for public office. But these God-given, legal and natural rights, as glorified either explicitly or implicitly in the Declaration of Independence, were denied to his older and wiser mother and grandmothers, and to the teachers or sisters and aunts who had taught him his Bible, his ABCs and Mother Goose rhymes.

And not so very long ago, a majority of the nine justices who constitute the United States Supreme Court were able to examine the Constitution and discover that it prescribed long prison terms at hard labor for indigent minors accused of a crime, an accusal which was tantamount to conviction because they lacked the access of a corporate executive to learned and expensive counsel. And the Supreme Court also approved of the separation of the races, and the arrest and imprisonment of political radicals, and the arrest of gays who believed they had a right to be sexually active in the privacy of their homes. And in January of 2010, in the case of *Citizens United v. Federal Election Commission*, the Supreme Court ruled in its wisdom and, by definition, supreme knowledge of the Constitution, that inanimate corporations were living persons with a constitutional right to exercise their freedom of speech and participate financially in the election process. Because money speaks louder than truth and facts in a political campaign, it is hard to believe that the Supreme Court was unaware that the domestic subsidiary of a multinational corporation that was secretly based in a communistic and atheistic state such as Russia or China will now and forever have more political power here than many a mainstream religious group or all the registered voters in Heartland states like Kansas or Iowa.

And before that, in 2000, five of the nine justices ignored the ancient legal doctrine of stare decisis and suddenly reversed decades of brilliant arguments on the Constitutional force majeure of states rights and discovered that the very same Constitution compelled them, and in no way setting a precedent, to hand down rulings in the Florida election dispute that was tantamount to their selection of George W. Bush as the forty-third President of the United States. We mention this Florida ruling, not at all to criticize or disagree but merely to point out that even the Supreme Court is subject to the winds of change, and such winds are never stronger than when they threaten to dislodge the political party to which a majority of our learned justices had once belonged and perhaps still do. Said English philosopher/statesman Francis Bacon (1561-1626), "He that will not apply new remedies must expect new evils." Francis Bacon was Lord Chancellor of England under James I, and, in days ahead, when we consider seniors and their growing threat, his words, beacons for the Founding Fathers, should now offer similar guidance to our three branches of government. In his *Advancement of Learning*, Lord Bacon endorsed the truism that was, is and always should be the guiding light for our leaders in both the public and private sectors: "All good moral philosophy is but the handmaid to religion." Lord Bacon's religion was surely a great comfort to him when, in 1621, after confessing to a charge of accepting bribes, he was fined, imprisoned for a time, and banished from Parliament and the royal court.

PRECONDITIONS FOR CHANGE

It is a very hard undertaking to please everyone.
Pubilius Syrus

Throughout a long career that culminated in his masterpiece, *The Enforcement of Morals*, Lord Patrick Arthur Devlin (1905-1992), perhaps Britain's most profound and respected legal scholar of the 20th Century, argued that private morality and behavior were a legitimate concern of the law and of government, the agent of the law. Therefore, in order to fulfill its duty to protect citizens, the state had a responsibility to determine and promote their best interests, *even against their wishes*. Were he still alive, Lord Devlin would surely approve wholeheartedly of our own government's disregard for the self-determination of citizens in such seemingly private matters as abortion and birth control, and suicide, and the use of narcotics, and indulgence in pornography and prostitution.

It is to be hoped that, in time, and with a few prods from public and private leaders and agencies that promote and finance faith-based initiatives, social forces will compel our religious bodies to apply the selective rational criteria that are so necessary for our times. And, having had their epiphanies with or without the guidance of their accountants and tax experts, shepherds of our various flocks, from Adventists to Unitarian Universalists and perhaps even Zen Buddhists, will withhold any objections to our proposed optimization of a population of seniors that has become as threatening to the future security of the nation as any foreign country or gang of terrorists can ever be. There are some clergy who might, to their credit, sermonize about universal *agape* and *caritas,* but we would respectfully remind them of the Christian tradition of sacrifice for others, beginning with the example of Jesus Himself upon the cross. And standard encyclopedias list the Christian martyrs of the following few centuries, from Saints Adelbert and Agatha to Saints Ursula and Vitus. All of which should impress upon our target audience that self-preservation may be the first law of our physical nature, but self-sacrifice is the first law of our transcendental nature and our kinship with the divine.

To deal with a seemingly insuperable obstacle such as the religious community, we hope to engage the services of a support team of senators, scholars, and opinion makers of the caliber and dedication that, for example, elevated Clarence Thomas to the Supreme Court in 1991. And the good news is that preliminary research informs us that many of his original supporters are more staunch and dedicated than ever to the principals we share. Though Justice Thomas was hailed by President George

H. W. Bush as the greatest legal mind in the country, and was supported by current Vice President Joseph Biden and other Democrats, there were critics who said that never in the history of the court did a candidate seem less qualified, and they even accused him of being less than truthful when he swore under oath to the Senate Judiciary Committee that he had never given a thought to the controversial subject of abortion, nor had he ever discussed it with fellow students at Yale Law School in 1973, when the Supreme Court announced its historic decision in *Roe v. Wade*. Nevertheless, as the country well knows, and to its great benefit, Justice Thomas overcame these obstacles and others, and he was able to realize his lifelong dream of becoming a Supreme Court justice and, as important, a role model to young African-Americans who might succumb to such lures as atheism, affirmative action and recreational sex. Let us hope that his support team have retained their notes and the strategy manuals that are known informally in their profession as the "little red idiot books."

Leaders of ethnic groups and racial and religious minorities will, of course, be assured that their followers will not be denied the privilege of participating in the Going Ahead program. Toward that desirable end, we will paraphrase the campaign slogan that President George W. Bush, employing the age-old doctrine of eminent domain, saw fit to preempt from the Children's Defense Fund, and we will declare at every opportunity in each of the fifty states: "Leave no senior behind!" And we would encourage friends in the media to deplore Jon Stewart, Stephen Colbert, Bill Maher and other so-called TV performers who might be tempted to revile our program with the words: "Leave no senior around!"

INITIATIVES

The windows of my soul I throw
Wide open to the sun.
Whittier

Advocates for what is truly best for our dearly beloved seniors have long dreamed of creating a new and more cost-effective program that will offer them a permanent escape from the boring and often painful activities of daily life. An escape from bathing, dressing, and cleaning their dentures and wigs. From keeping track of their shelves of medications and their appointments with doctors of every classification in the *Merck Manual of Medical Information*. From cooking and from cleaning house. From weeding gardens and shoveling snow. From dependency upon others for transportation to houses of worship, public libraries and museums, supermarkets and shopping malls. From the shock and increased hypertension of, for example, learning that a physical therapist has billed Medicare $150 for ten minutes of instruction on hand exercises that are free on the Internet or in the public library.

The backward philosophy and lack of discipline of all too many of our political, religious and cultural leaders must be changed, and if they do not respond readily, and without whining, to the usual carrots of campaign money and lucrative employment in the private or public sectors for themselves and family, and for friends and lovers, then it will have to be done with such traditional sticks as the (1) financing and glorification of rival politicians, (2) the exposure of their womanizing and over-indulgence of pork, and (3) their immoderate demands for what was once called graft but is now garbed in such euphemisms as "constituent service" and "enhanced communication."

Ordinarily, members of a task force can roll up their sleeves and go right to work on an assigned problem. If the problem, for example, be the securing of tax exemptions for alleged nonprofit groups or the elimination of anachronistic zoning laws that limit the size of industrial parks and shopping malls, we know by now, as law-abiding citizens in a democracy, that we must engage more and better lawyers and lobbyists than our opponents, increase campaign contributions to legislators, employ the spouses and relatives of judges, and ingratiate ourselves with the media and power brokers. In the present instance, however, the problem being a permanent and cost-effective transposition of the nonproductive seniors in our midst, enough of them to clog the economic engine that drives the nation, our first and greatest task is to overcome a severe misconception on the part of the American public about the true nature of suicide.

Perceived within a patriotic context, the traditional concept of suicide, "the taking of one's own life by a person of sound mind," is to be deconstructed to the point of irrelevancy, and to be replaced by the positive phrase "Going Ahead," which will denote a scheduled self-termination and connote a transition to a more desirable realm of being. According to taste, as it were, it might be to an eternity of vacationing in the Caribbean. Or of drinking beer and sitting in the VIP section of a baseball or football stadium. Here is a charming insight by the Reverend Henry Ward Beecher (1813-1887): "To us who are Christians, is it not a solemn, but a delightful thought, that perhaps nothing but the opaque bodily eye prevents us from beholding the gate which is open just before us: and nothing but the dull ear prevents us from hearing the ringing of those bells of joy, which welcome us to the heavenly land?" It is surely superfluous to mention that the Reverend Beecher, having survived an adultery scandal with an attractive congregant, was hailed in his day as the most eloquent clergyman in Brooklyn, then known for its abundance of churches rather than of bagel bakeries and pizza restaurants.

Admittedly, the phrase "scheduled self-termination" does not come trippingly to the tongue or pleasingly to the ear, but Dr. Bowers, our in-house rhetorician, is confident that after a brief period of public exposure it will sound as natural as such a formerly awkward phrase as, "a Starbucks mocha with a double of low-fat caramel-flavored whipped cream and a side order of Oreo cookies with mint peanut butter crème." After a two-week brainstorming conference at a chalet on an island in Lake Lucerne, and very kindly provided by an international banking consortium that has often availed itself of our services, Seneca experts have come to believe that the initial targets of our educational program should be (1) outmoded sectors of the legal system and (2) institutions and individuals who are well-meaning in their loyalty to the teachings of their religion but are living in a past when, to risk sounding flippant, spiritual wealth trumped material wealth, and when loaves and fishes, and wine and water, were the joys of man's nutritional desiring. As all the world knows, the late William F. Buckley Jr. was a devout Catholic and the inspiration for dozens of conservative and neoconservative groups, among them the Federalist Society and Tea Party. But as he grew older and, incredibly, even wiser than in his senior year at Yale, he changed his views of a lifetime and called increasingly for a reassessment of what he perceived as the country's failed and cost-ineffective policy on narcotics. Were Mr. Buckley still alive, we like to think that he would give a fair hearing to and eventually approve of our program. Surely, like his friend Pope John Paul II, Mr. Buckley agreed with the eternal truth of John 15:13: "Greater love hath no man than this, that a man lay down his life for his friends."

Hy Brett

All over the world, whether they be average Eskimos in Alaska or average, hardworking stockbrokers on Wall Street, and no occupation works harder for its daily bread, members of the species Homo sapiens experience the same twists and turns of the life cycle: the meeting and interaction of sperm and egg, fetushood and the ever-present threats of abortion and miscarriage, infancy and childhood, puberty and mating; pregnancy and menopause in women; erectile dysfunction in men; aging, senility, and finally death. But there is great variation in the personal and social values assigned to the various stages and their enactment. The modern-day notion that seniors, regardless of their health and finances, must be assisted by the state in living as long as possible, even if that living, like in the case of brain-damaged Terri Schiavo, be in a coma for fifteen years and dependent upon costly technology, is as harmful to senior patients as it is to society.

The sober, pragmatic, and socially responsible truth is that there comes a time for seniors to realize, or, in a spirit of altruism and love, be conditioned to realize that they have partaken of their allotted time on earth and that they should and they must participate in the patriotic ceremony of Going Ahead. Their time for closure is at hand, and they must comprehend that it is a joyful time, and as natural to the life cycle as birth and all the intervening ages and stages. By Going Ahead, seniors would make way for their juniors, the men and women whose work and expenditures for goods and services, whose investments

54

and taxes, sustain rather than drain our beloved country. Not unlike manufacturers with even their top-of-the-line coffee makers and toasters and dishwashers, Nature has seen fit and proper to build an obsolescence into humanity. From Psalm 90:10 we learn straight from the shoulder, and with the bluntness of the stone that David directed at Goliath, a profound truth about humans, whether in biblical times or in America in the twenty-first century: "The days of our years are threescore years and ten; and if by reason of strength they be fourscore years, yet is their strength labor and sorrow, and we fly away."

COMPENSATION TO HEALTH CARE INDUSTRY

Justice and good will outlast passion.
President James A. Garfield

Being firmly committed to the free-market system that has made our nation the greatest on earth, Seneca believes that an equitable compensation must be made to the health care industry for depriving it of the well-earned profits of their employment of ever more advanced technology to prolong the comas and lives of seniors and super-seniors, who, without our intervention, would constitute at least 20 percent of the population by 2050. Since the inception of Medicaid and Medicare in 1965, drug companies, hospitals and medical groups, most of them financial supporters of the major parties in Washington, have expected to receive a good part of their income from their prescribing of long-term, life-sustaining procedures for seniors, even when the procedures were often against the wishes of well-meaning but misguided patients and immediate family. In order to avoid resistance to the Going Ahead Program by the medical establishment and its lobbyists, many of them former and future government officials, we would advise our friends in Congress to secretly guarantee compensation to our health care friends by insinuating appropriate loopholes into future legislation, whether it be for development of space weapons or for the relaxation of corporate responsibility for air pollution. This guaranteed income should be no more objectionable to true conservatives than the sort of tax relief that is extended by every Congress to individual and corporate supporters.

To justify this guaranteed income that would protect the anticipated profits of the health care industry, Seneca through its contacts in the medical and academic communities will encourage ongoing research that, for example, discovers the physical, mental, and emotional benefits to younger citizens of penile enlargement for males and breast enhancement for females. Reports on television and in the print media will tell of men and women who have achieved greater income, self-esteem and popularity through their increased length and girth. On the Discovery Channel, for instance, a documentary hosted by a male and female beneficiary of the procedure will report on entertainers and business leaders whose careers did not take off until after their physical enhancements. In all cases, the real and enduring reward of their careers will be not a contract to perform in Las Vegas or to head General Electric but the opportunity to become a more active participant in the President's clarion call for a return to the family values of America's glorious past. Whether or not Arnold Schwarzenegger and Dolly Parton ever had such surgery, they could render a unique service to the country by becoming spokespersons for Bigger Is Better.

FRAMING

The appearance of things is deceptive.
Seneca

In 1994, when President Bill Clinton and his First Lady proposed a legislative monstrosity that purported to provide universal health coverage for the nation, their machinations were successfully framed by opponents in the health-care industry as a bureaucratic assault upon the sanctity of the patient-doctor relationship, without which invalids would never again arise from their sickbeds. Once the Clintons were defeated, health insurers and health maintenance organizations hastened to establish themselves as arbitrators of the hallowed patient-doctor relationship, to the extent of overriding doctors' recommendations that might diminish their bottom lines and violate their primary responsibility, which was to shareholders. Here and there in his works, the late Milton Friedman, noted economist and Nobel laureate, has many a wise word to say about business organizations and their limited or lack of responsibility to extra-economic institutions, including charities. "The social responsibility of business," he said like a true patriot, "is to increase profits."

Year after year, decade after decade, the National Rifle Association, gun makers and gun dealers have framed the possession of ever more technically advanced firearms as a constitutional right under the Second Amendment, and so basic to the welfare of the Republic that it is the very foundation of all our other rights. The National Rifle Association has been so successful over the decades that, if asked or ordered to do so, its beneficiaries on Capitol Hill and along other corridors of power would surely support a bill that justified the possession of guided missiles as necessary for the hunting of rabbits, not to mention deer and wolves.

In 1998 the tobacco industry framed antismoking legislation, intended to benefit public health and decrease the cost of Medicaid and Medicare, as a violation of consumer rights and a tax increase upon smokers. The following year, we learned from a report in *The New York Times* that the lobbyists of the National Restaurant Association are disposed to frame their arguments not in terms that would suggest self-interest but as constitutional concerns that are far away from their perfectly legitimate mission, which is to create and sustain a milieu favorable to the sale of such dietary staples as steaks and hamburgers.

We must act upon the lessons learned from the above frames, and, therefore, our frame for reducing and eventually eliminating senior expenditures must, at a minimum, incorporate the positive elements in the campaign rhetoric of both Republicans and Democrats in the year 2012. We must emphasize the continuation of the American Way of Life, the ever-popular benefits to children and grandchildren, the protection of family values and the free market system, the provision of more and better jobs, greater security against foreign states and foreign and domestic terrorists. To obtain the participation of the gay community, we will remain silent on the still controversial subject of same-sex marriage. But we will very definitely urge our contacts in the Right to Life community to continue to concentrate on the sacred and legal rights of the unborn, and to cease all activities that might publicize the so-called rights of seniors. In the late summer of 2011, during a presidential primary debate by Republican Party contenders, we were heartened by the applause for Texas Governor Rick Perry's defense of the 234 executions during his tenure. And also, during the televised debate before an audience, we were deeply moved and inspired by the loud applause when a contender mentioned that death might be an option for Americans who lacked health insurance and could not keep up with their financial responsibilities.

The public must be conditioned to believe, and to believe with the passion of sports fans for the most mediocre of teams, that all over America children are being denied their birthright of a world-class education in a top-rated school, and the reason for the deprivation is that senior citizens and their powerful lobbyists have succeeded for decades in misappropriating an unconscionable proportion of public funds. Further, that because of the greed and callousness of seniors, the future guardians of our beloved country are dying of disease and malnutrition. For example, it may be alleged during flu season that precious and life-saving vaccines are being diverted from nurseries to nursing homes. To be sure, once our proposals are in force and money is diverted from seniors, a certain portion of the savings will very definitely be spent upon the aforementioned children, but the bulk of the money will be returned, and perhaps even with retroactive interest, to individuals and corporations that have been overtaxed over the decades.

THE ROAD TO THE FUTURE

A word to the wise needs no disguise,
But words to the rabble need ever more babble.
Claude Bridges *(after Horace)*

What follows below is a comprehensive educational/ promotional/communications program that has been created by Seneca Research and Development Associates for later execution by an action affiliate to be called perhaps Sunshine Sendoffs. Our studies indicate that our goals can be achieved by the year 2019 or even sooner, depending (1) upon the presidential, congressional, and state election results of the intervening years, and (2) whether it becomes necessary to acquire the expensive but effective services of lobbying and consulting firms of the stature of the BGR Group, which works with Fortune 500 companies, governments and worthy enterprises like your own. You may rest assured that, if requested by our clients in Washington, Seneca can devise a strategy for a positive outcome of all relevant elections, and not only in Florida, where, in the contentious year 2000, as mentioned before, we finally had to come to the rescue of our clients and arrange for the cooperation, whether they were aware of it or not, of five justices of the United States Supreme Court. "*Salus populi suprema lex,*" said Cicero, the Roman statesman. The safety of the people is the highest law. [For more on this sensitive subject, please see Operation Al below, to be found in Appendix B.]

We are proud and delighted to inform you that our suggested program has been approved unanimously, and with unprecedented speed and enthusiasm, by a specially selected panel of senior fellows at Seneca. They are men and women who have been professionally trained in sensitivity at leading institutes and therefore understand the classic techniques and procedures for maintaining the dignity and self-respect of the seniors who will be subjected to our education process and then be processed accordingly. After sub rosa consultation with trustworthy colleagues who are either faith based, faith neutral or faith negative, Professor Avery F. Sawyer, our bioethicist, is confident that the Program, when in full swing, will be interpreted by right-minded Americans to fall well within the parameters of the moral guidelines of all major and most minor religions. He is particularly pleased with the approval of his mentor, Professor Fritz C. Hansell, who has been associated with universities the world over, and is currently on leave from his post at the Adolf Gottwald Institute of Strategic Interaction, the Munich-based think tank that has advised all German leaders since Chancellor Otto von Bismarck (1815-1898). Among recent assignments of Professor

Hansell was a determination of whether nine was a suitable minimum age for female labor in jogging-shoe factories in Southeast Asia. After studying the socioeconomic conditions in that part of the world, and aware of how they differed from conditions in America, he recommended that the minimum age should be no earlier than nine years and seven months, and his views were eventually adopted by his client, the Southeast Asia-American Association of Leisure Shoe and Slipper Manufacturers. He was even able to prevail upon his client to permit up to six bathroom visits totaling ten minutes per child per working week of six days. After tsunamis and the inevitable epidemics of dysentery and other gastrointestinal afflictions, the schedule of bathroom visits would be adjusted on an ad hoc basis.

Among the most effective of our educational assets will be current leaders of the mainstream religions, and we expect them to cooperate fully with our program, if not immediately then after interaction with our Commission on Guidance and Special Education. In the unlikely event that they do not cooperate, and we would certainly understand and sympathize with their adherence to the alleged traditions of their forefathers, we will have no choice not only to review their tax responsibilities but also to begin a parallel and more responsive religious movement, one headed by a figure whom we will develop into a role model of truth, love and piety. Such figures should be readily at hand in the persons of recently retired athletes, actors and rock stars.

THE THREE SCORE AND TEN SOCIETY

Don't let the fear of striking out hold you back.
Babe Ruth

We are convinced that fundamentalists and other true believers in a literal rather than a merely symbolic interpretation of Scripture will eventually be persuaded to join and adhere to the precepts of our contemplated Three Score and Ten Society. Truly, if they be not hypocrites and deserving of excommunication and an eternity in hell, they will have no moral choice but to join the society and follow its precepts, just as they currently follow, or profess to follow, and to their credit, such other pious precepts as creationism, premarital chastity, fetal protection, and the unification of church and state. To be sure, the ideal leader of the society would be a respected man or woman who would set a shining example for his/her millions of admirers and participate in a Going Ahead ceremony that would be televised across the country. Since it is uncertain whether, despite their true-and-tried patriotism, former New York City Mayor Rudolph Giuliani and former First Lady Laura Bush would accept such leadership roles in the foreseeable future, we must find a fundamentalist whom we can develop into a role model of the eminence of Mr. Giuliani and the former First Lady. Using the mailing list provided by a Seneca trustee who is also a high official of the American Guild of Advertising and Public Relations Executives, we have performed a dry run, as it were, and discovered to our delight that we already have 1,007 candidates with an infinite diversity of faces, figures, handshakes and hairdos, ethnic backgrounds and personality profiles available for the role. Should, after our time and effort on his/her behalf, our chosen fundamentalist have a change of heart at the last moment and prefer to continue life as a leader of a popular and lucrative enterprise, which may well happen, we are confident that friends in the FBI and IRS, and also contractors in the private sector will find ways of restoring the purity of his/her original faith.

Also, while on the subject of religion, one of our top priorities must be the formation of an ecumenical grass-roots movement called, perhaps, Glory for Geriatrics. With the abundance of cynicism abroad in the land, even a dubious enterprise must be dressed up in spiritual finery these days, but, of course, Glory for Geriatrics will be on the entirely pure and credible end of the moral spectrum. As Shakespeare would have said of us, "There's nothing ill can dwell in such a temple." By a stroke of good fortune, a consulting firm headed by one of our trustees has recently interviewed a diversity of churchmen on behalf of a Wall

Street investment bank that is sublimating its public image after newspaper accounts of its deep involvement in the creation of sixty-one tax-free corporate subsidiaries based in the Cayman Islands. Our trustee is confident that his Wall Street client will be happy to share his research with us.

THE SOCIAL CONSTRUCTION AND
RECONSTRUCTION OF GERIATRIC SCENARIOS

Nothing can be created out of nothing.
Lucretius

According to poll after poll, eight out of ten Americans believe that the grave is not the end, and that an afterlife awaits them. Further, they believe that the afterlife will be a pleasant life, both absolutely and in comparison to their life on earth, even though it was lived in the greatest country that ever existed on this or any other planet in the solar system. Or even in the entire cosmos. But, rather perversely, very few of those same people are eager to leave their present world with all of its taxes, aches and pains, perfidious politicians and other tribulation.

To energize these procrastinators who would delay the inevitable, we would strongly recommend the commissioning of a book about the afterlife, and in our book not a word about the death process, a negative concept, will be mentioned. On the contrary, we will be depicting and glorifying rebirth, a rebirth to eternal life, and nothing could be more positive and beneficial than that.

For not a day longer will the virtuous have to wait to see their enemies suffering in hell. Spirits of the departed will return regularly to earth for updates on the activities of family, friends, pets, entertainers, and sports events such as the World Series and the Super Bowl. Being spirits and incorporeal, they can be present in Scotland and witness their favorite golfer win a British Open. And then, in a flash, if the two events coincide, they can be across the English Channel and witness their favorite cyclist win the Tour de France, hopefully without the benefit of drugs.

But seniors must first be convinced that they are currently being deprived of an important right, the right to conclude their own life on earth and get on the fast track to a better life in the beyond. This can be their final act of patriotism, one as glorious as death on a battlefield in Iraq or Afghanistan or any future combat zone. Nearly forty states have statutes that force the mentally ill into treatment against their will. Even libertarians will agree that educating the elderly about the option of Going Ahead is far less authoritarian than forcing treatment upon the mentally ill, or imprisoning a citizen for possessing a tiny amount of marijuana, a substance no more harmful than alcohol, an addictive drug that, though responsible for millions of physical and mental ailments a year, and tens of thousands of auto accidents every year, is perfectly legal and is consumed daily and perhaps hourly by members of our three branches of government.

Our first objective will be to create a climate of opinion in which Americans will reverse their current beliefs and come to regard scheduled self-termination by seniors as a virtue and not a sin or a crime. They will come to agree wholeheartedly with the Reverend Henry Ward Beecher, Brooklyn's golden orator of yesteryear, that "There is no unmixed good in this world except dying." And they will agree with an equally wise English thinker, the Reverend Charles C. Colton, previously quoted, that "Death is the liberator of him whom freedom cannot release, the physician of him whom medicine cannot cure, and the comforter of him whom time cannot console."

Though the overwhelming number of Americans believe that the Bible is the true word of God, most of them, including members of the three branches of government, have learned the wisdom of good old American pragmatism, and are inclined to pick and choose among biblical precepts. Court witnesses, before offering testimony, must swear upon the Bible, even though, according to Matthew 5:34-35, Jesus forbids swearing. In the following verses of the same chapter, Jesus urges his listeners to resist not evil, and to love enemies, and to forgive debtors, and to lay not up treasures upon earth, and not to judge others, and to give to him who asks of thee. How many Americans, even those who call themselves fundamentalists, adhere strictly to these noble but unrealistic teachings? If they did, far more havoc would be created than by the mere self-termination of seniors.

Ever since the 13th century, the Catholic Church and the Orthodox Churches have officially authorized only seven sacraments: baptism, confirmation, Eucharist, penance, extreme unction, Holy Orders, and marriage. Protestant Churches no longer consider marriage to be a sacrament, but they, like the Catholic and Orthodox Church, and all branches of Judaism, stipulate marriage vows that include the promise to love and to cherish, for better and for worse, for richer and for poorer, in sickness and in health, until parted by death. And the marriage cannot be valid until a clergyman or judge has asked of the bride and the groom if they make this lifelong promise to each other, and each has responded, "I do." Nevertheless, the most recent census reports that 9.9 percent of the population has had at least one divorce. Included in those figures, and few Americans hold it against them, are such icons and role models as President Ronald Reagan, former New York City Mayors Rudy Giuliani and Michael Bloomberg, House Speaker Newt Gingrich and New York State Governor Andrew Cuomo. And few are the pious baseball fans who object to the two divorces—from Dorothy Arnold in 1944 and Marilyn Monroe in 1954—of Joe DiMaggio. To his credit, Academy Award winner Spencer Tracy, a Catholic, remained true to his marital vows during his long relationship with superstar Katharine Hepburn.

CHANNELS OF INFORMATION

*The people may be made to follow a path of
action, but they may not be made
to understand it.*

Confucius

High on our agenda will be the creation of a nationwide grass-roots organization to be called Partnership for Sunshine Sendoffs, or perhaps Americans United for Sunshine Sendoffs. Our strong preference for grass-roots activity is influenced by the philosophy of President Herbert Hoover, who believed that "No governmental action, no economic doctrine, no economic plan or project can replace that God-imposed responsibility of the individual man and woman to their [sic] neighbors."

By special arrangement with telephone companies across the land, the organization will have a toll-free number, 1-555-USA-SENIORS, for the questions and problems of departing seniors and their families. Further, we strongly suggest that our friends in both the public and private sectors use their influence to assure that Dane V. Beattley, founder of True Voices from the Heartland, be appointed to head and organize our grass-roots organization. Most if not all of you know of Mr. Beattley's work, and over the years, when other remedies failed, you may even have availed yourself of his unique services. Abortion, gun control, school prayer and school busing, affirmative action, self-regulation for industry, stock options for CEO's—on both sides of these important and controversial issues, often both sides concurrently, he and his staff of experts have rallied their countrymen and motivated them to crystallize and express their views to the media and public servants in Washington and state capitals across the land. A tobacco executive who prefers anonymity said recently, "I strongly believe that with Dane's solid contacts with the media and the research industry, he is fully capable of having cigarettes perceived as a health food by the public. And the tobacco industry may yet decide upon such a defensive measure if other cities follow the example of New York, where the tax rises every time a mayor enters a public place and is offended by second-hand smoke. My daddy, may he rest in peace, recalled the good old days when cigarettes cost fifteen cents a pack and were endorsed by such great American icons as Joe DiMaggio and Ronald Reagan as an aid to relaxation and better performance on the job."

On July 9, 2002, *The Wall Street Journal* reported that the AAHP, the American Association of Health Plans, would pay the legendary William Morris talent agency "an undisclosed sum for access to key writers, power brokers and directors as well as for advance word about coming movies and television shows that might paint the insurers in a bad light." The AAHP hoped, of course, to influence how they would be portrayed in the visual media, and that, certainly, is a fundamental right in a free country such as ours. Needless to say, the AAHP received the excellent results that our own enterprise expects from either William Morris or any other top-flight agency that we would be considering for similar work in behalf of Operation Going Ahead. Should we, for example, be informed of plans for yet another sequel to *Jurassic Park*, we would contact Oscar-winning filmmaker Steven Spielberg and suggest that younger members of an expedition be saved from the prehistoric beasts by the self-sacrifice of a heroic senior, played perhaps by Clint Eastwood, born in 1930, or by Robert Redford, born in 1936. The same would be true for sequels to such popular films and TV programs as *The Sopranos, The Mummy*, and *101 Dalmatians*. In the last-named, a plucky senior played by Debbie Reynolds, born in 1932, would die after rescuing the adorable Dalmatians from a rabid wolfhound in the employ of Cruella de Ville, played with her usual malevolence by Glenn Close, born in 1947.

On a related line of endeavor, we have already been assured of the services of Caroline's Original Celebrity Development and Supply Company, the Beverly Hills firm that provides both celebrities and under-appreciated people of distinction—e.g., champions in the consumption of bagels, burgers and bran muffins—to radio and television talk shows in all the fifty states and as far away as Japan. Our contact at Caroline's Celebrity will engage the aforementioned would-be celebrities who, in return for exposure on *Today* or *The Tonight Show* will popularize our views on public service, senior responsibilities and the death experience. Please see Appendix F for an example of how popular TV personality Katie Couric might, without even her foreknowledge, further our cause in an interview with an author who supports Going Ahead.

OBITER DICTUM

Belief is the death of intelligence.
Robert Anton Wilson

At this point in our report, some readers may be surprised if not puzzled by our occasional deviation from solid facts and statistics, the standard material of such reports, to the discussion of such seemingly marginal material as radio and television interviews. Let those readers be forewarned that they may encounter even more surprises in pages to come, which deal with suggested strategies for inducing seniors to participate in the Going Ahead Program. We are fully aware that these techniques may be perceived as "pushing the envelope" to the edge of credibility. But readers of this report, who are all highly educated men and women, must be well aware by now that the target audience for our product will be coming from very different strata of society than themselves, and will have different tastes and beliefs, different lifestyles and, let us be candid among ourselves, far different intelligence quotients, even ones that cannot be measured.

For the most part, our target subculture is comprised

of people, the Good Lord bless them, who lack college or perhaps even high school diplomas, and who read only the celebrity gossip and sports section in their newspaper, if they read a newspaper at all. They march in parades and attend rallies where they applaud and cheer the twaddle that speechmakers are almost ashamed to write for candidates who struggle to suppress a grin as they read from their idiot cards or teleprompters. They are amenable to the influence of significant others—entertainers, political and sports figures, cartoon characters—whom they know only through the mass media and handshake opportunities. They are the so-called average Americans who watch television to excess—reality shows and situation comedies, political conventions and State of the Union addresses, football games and baseball games, cooking shows and interviews with celebrities known only to their press agents and their immediate families and their dogs. With unquestioning faith in their leaders and system of government, they, our target audience of both seniors and pre-seniors, paid the estimated $300 billion of their taxes which in the 1980s bailed out the savings and loan banks whose risky investments, often tantamount to legal larceny, were made possible and were even encouraged as good business by President Reagan and congressmen in both parties. During the next presidential campaign, citizens did not protest or question the lid of silence placed on this malfeasance by both Washington and the media. Instead, they were diverted and incensed by the GOP's claim that Democratic candidate Michael Dukakis was responsible for the criminality of Willie Horton, a charge later admitted to be false and cruel by his opponent's campaign consultant, Lee Atwater, as he lay on his deathbed.

On March 23, 2009, Treasury Secretary Timothy Geithner, a favorite financial guru of both the Bush and Obama administrations, announced that the federal government would buy up to a half-trillion dollars in toxic assets that had been accumulated by megabanks during the housing bubble. The toxic assets, some awarded an AAA, its highest rating, by Standard & Poor's, were bundles of mostly subprime mortgages that had been traded back and forth on Wall Street. The trades had been profitable both for the banks and their top brass, but were now revealed to be worth only a fraction of their alleged and anticipated value. The banks were rescued thanks to the money that citizens had been taxed to pay for the more usual and vital services of their federal government. Deprived of these services for the foreseeable future, millions upon millions of hard-working Americans were to lose their homes, savings and jobs, their hopes for a brighter future for themselves and their families. And yet there was no backlash worthy of the name by the public. In fact, during the congressional elections of 2010, the party favored by the banks and big corporations won back control of the House of Representatives from the Democrats, the party that favored the traditional and popular entitlements for low- and middle-class citizens. We at Seneca submit, and we are sure you will agree, that after a lifetime of their exposure to our socio-cultural verities, no envelope can be pushed too far for the true believers in our midst, and that they will accept our programs to their death. Or should we say, rather, to their Going Ahead?

SPOKESPERSONS

Hitch your wagon to a star.
Emerson

Institutions both commercial and governmental have come to realize that in their relations with the public, nothing is more important than a spokesperson who symbolizes all the alleged values and benefits of the product or ideology. For our own purpose, which is the encouragement of the voluntary scheduling of self-termination, the ideal choice would be a beloved and compelling couple—husband and wife, preferably—who are reminiscent of Lucille Ball and Desi Arnaz at the peak of their popularity on television. Once upon a time, their later divorce would have invalidated them as spokespersons, but the divorces of such vocal champions of family values as Ronald Reagan and Newt Gingrich have caused their admirers to identify and valorize one of the positive aspects of divorce: namely, that it may be a vital stage in an ongoing search for the ultimate in family values, and what is more valuable in a family than a compatible spouse? According to Roman philosopher Cicero (106-43 B.C.) at a time when he may have been thinking about marriage, "Any man may make a mistake, but only a fool will continue in it." Cicero made no mistake in his own marriage. A recent English biographer, D. R. Shackleton Bailey, says of Cicero's wife, Terentia, "There is no record of her age or looks, but she was certainly rich and well-connected."

Currently, our experts are considering the qualifications of six couples of varying celebrity on its short list of candidates for spokespersons. Among the front-runners are Linda and Hal Harvety, both 58, and both from Friendly Valley, Oklahoma, which boasts of being important enough to have a Walmart within only fifty-eight miles from its town hall. After a successful career in residential and commercial real estate, they opted for early retirement, but they soon realized that more important than retirement to them was their desire to continue to serve their friends and neighbors. And so, lifelong champions of the First Amendment, they are now enjoying a second and even more rewarding career as professional organizers of spontaneous protests. On behalf of an organization of vegetarians in their state, Linda and Hal are currently organizing a protest against fast-food restaurants that serve hamburgers and hot dogs. This assignment is a counterattack against a previous one in which, on behalf of a consortium of meat packers, they organized a statewide protest against vegetarian restaurants, claiming, as their keynote, that a deficiency of meat in the American diet will lead to a loss of the courage and fighting spirit that have sustained our freedom since 1776. With this wealth of practical experience, Hal and Linda are an ideal choice to, for example, organize a spontaneous demonstration at the home and/or headquarters of a manufacturer of apparatus that sustains the life of comatose seniors who are not expected to recover and meanwhile are draining Medicare.

Thanks to the efforts of the Harvetys and to the efforts also of their daughters Nancy and Laura, named for the wives of President Reagan and President Bush respectively, high school virgins now outnumber sexually active students by 94 percent to 6 percent in Friendly Valley. Ten years ago, these numbers were reversed! Teenage pregnancy and births have also dropped dramatically!

GRIEF COUNSELING

Those whom true love has held,
it will go on holding.
Seneca

Thanks to multimedia programs that will employ the latest advances in digital computing, we fully expect the Going Ahead of seniors to be a totally joyful occasion for family and friends. In fact, we expect a number 10 on the Happy Day scale invented by Dr. Irma Weelmeyer of the Harvard Medical School, as reported in the spring 2011 issue of *The Journal of Interactive Personality Dynamics*. For family members and friends who remain skeptical of the program and its many benefits, and who still take the old-fashioned view that scheduled voluntary termination for seniors is undesirable or even sinful, we will suggest a regimen of sedatives and/or a course of treatment with a qualified grief counselor who shares the ideals of the Going Ahead program. So that the counseling process will be as financially painless as possible, we will contact the National Association of Board-Certified Grief Counselors and make every effort to arrange a discount rate for family and friends of the departed. Family and friends who itemize their medical expenses will be further pleased to learn that, according to our contact at the Internal Revenue Service, fees for grief counseling will be as deductible as their fees for medical and dental procedures.

BELIEF DEVELOPMENT AGENCY

*Credulous hope supports our life, and always
says that tomorrow will be better.*
Tibullus

A high priority for Sunshine Sendoffs will be the establishment of a Belief Development Agency. Totally dedicated to impacting the lives of seniors in a positive way, its mission will be the production of favorable books, magazine articles, and television documentaries on the subject of scheduled voluntary self-termination in general and of such famous and diverse terminators in particular as the Roman philosopher-statesman Seneca; Greek philosopher Socrates; artists Vincent Van Gogh, Ray Johnson and Mark Rothko; authors Anne Sexton, Hart Craine, Ernest Hemingway, Jerzy Kosinski, Sylvia Plath and Virginia Woolf; inventor-philanthropist George Eastman; screen stars George Sanders and Charles Boyer; Carthaginian general Hannibal; and German Field Marshal Ernest Rommel. Of interest to both music lovers and feminists, even though she did not self-terminate, will be a biography of Sarah Flower Adams, author of "Nearer, My God, to Thee."

We also suggest the eventual establishment at a prominent institution in Washington, perhaps the Smithsonian, of a Self-Terminator's Hall of Fame. Though famous only in their own hometown, each self-terminator will be honored with his/her name on a wall in the grand lobby. Admittance to The Self-Terminator's Hall of Fame will be free of charge for seniors and their immediate family, and we believe that an optimum location for an information booth for the Going Ahead program should be equidistant on the main floor between the lunchroom and restroom. At an early date we will commission an ethicist of national repute to write a work to be called, perhaps, *The Moral Basis of Senior Self-Termination*. Former Secretary of Education William J. Bennett would be ideal for the assignment. At present, Mr. Bennett, a devout Catholic and leader in the Right to Life movement, is surely opposed to senior self-termination, and we, his longtime admirers, certainly respect his opinion. But on the other hand, his silence on such issues as capital punishment in Texas and other states where defendants receive not the best of legal counsel, and his silence on the feeble gun controls that result yearly in thousands of deaths, many of them innocent women and children, leads us to believe that his opposition to the self-termination of seniors may not be absolute, and that he may see his way to obeying the command of Jesus in Matthew 22:21 and "Render therefore unto Caesar the things which are Caesar's."

Should Mr. Bennett have any further doubts about

the ethical aspects of Going Ahead and its possible conflict with the sixth of the Ten Commandments in the Holy Bible, he may be heartened by the example of former President George W. Bush, who took pride of in having repented of the sins of his youth and becoming a Born Again Christian. While governor of the Lone Star State, Mr. Bush permitted 152 executions that were in his power to prevent. In the case of Karla Faye Tucker, executed on February 3, 1998, Governor Bush ignored appeals for clemency by people all over the country and the world, including evangelists Pat Robertson and Jerry Falwell. And even by Pope John Paul II, often called the moral leader of the world. However, being a compassionate conservative, Governor Bush did ask of God that He bless Karla Faye Tucker. And what sinner about to leave this world could ask for more?

Perhaps the original and most profound inspiration of the conservative and neoconservative movements in the United States has been Irish-British statesman, orator and political theorist Edmund Burke (1729-97) and here are his thoughts on change: "If a great change is to be made in human affairs, the minds of men will be fitted to it; the general feelings and opinions will draw that way. Every fear and hope will forward it; and they who persist in opposing this mighty current will appear rather to resist the decrees of Providence itself than the mere designs of men. They will not be so much resolute and firm as perverse and obstinate."

Our author, an undisputed world-class ethicist, will emphasize how past societies dealt, to their great advantage, with a surfeit of indigent seniors. Though self-termination is considered a sin by Judaism, Christianity and Islam, it has enough popular appeal to have become the eighth leading cause of the death process in our country, with seniors of sixty-five and over accounting for 19 percent of the category. No less an authority than John Shelby Spong, retired Episcopal bishop of Newark, has written that the words of the Bible "are always limited by their time, their culture, and their apprehension of reality."

As is well known to scholars, senior self-termination is not a new idea but an old and honorable one whose time has come again, and with greater urgency than ever before. Scholars inform us that a right-to-die movement was flourishing in ancient Greece, a country that, like our own, gloried in a free market system. The Greeks could also boast of their art, drama and the think tanks of Plato and Aristotle, as well as democracy for male aristocrats, and of Olympic games, and of enslaving rather than totally slaughtering the populations of conquered city-states. And of a style of architecture that was to achieve perfection in our own White House and Capitol building. True, the Greeks imposed slavery upon much of their population, but so did the United States at one time practice slavery, and also displace and/or eliminate Native Americans and Mexicans in Texas and the Southwest. But to paraphrase Jesus, "That country which is or ever was without slavery in one form or another, let it cast the first vote at the United Nations Human Rights Commission."

People over seventy-five have the highest self-termination rate in the United States, and gerontologists attribute it to depression caused by the downgrading of their social roles and the daily grind of coping with physical weakness. In *Suicide,* his seminal and still authoritative work, French sociologist Emile Durkheim wrote in 1897 of the relentless conflict between individuals and the rapidly changing societies which they had no choice but to inhabit. Admittedly, in our own society, wealthy seniors retain the power to ease their lives with servants, and toy boys and trophy wives, and the companionship of kindly kin and friends who have hopes of an inheritance. They have access to transportation and a more congenial environment in another state or country. They enjoy the latest in home and outdoor appliances. After generous contributions to political campaigns, they can avail themselves of such supreme life-enhancing experiences as mingling with a President and First Lady at a fund-raiser or at the White House. They can even move to another country, perhaps la belle France or sunny Spain, where they will save on taxes and still be entitled to their Social Security checks and to Medicare. On the other hand, the poor in America do retain the power to end their lives, and according to our contacts in the hospice movement, their last words often express a yearning to be rewarded in the hereafter for service to their country or a favorite cause.

Therefore, our in-house educators and affiliated pundits will frame their products around national well-being and personal glorification. We will inform seniors of the findings of economist Mancur Olson, author of *Power and Prosperity*, who, in his comprehensive study of a stagnant Japanese economy, observed that nations lose their vitality because seniors and other special interests seize and hold on to entitlements that are detrimental to other groups.

When inculcated early enough, Going Ahead, as mentioned before and cannot be repeated too often, would be regarded as much a public duty as voting, paying taxes, jury duty, and military service. According to a special and secret panel of the National Association of Board-Certified Ethicists and Marriage/Divorce Counselors, all of whose members desire anonymity at the present time, what we propose in this presentation is an effective and also humane way of dealing with the vast majority of dysfunctional seniors. We recognize that our proposals may be misconstrued as a manifestation of ill-will and even cruelty, and we foresee a high volume and intensity of public outrage that will be orchestrated by the interest groups which gorge themselves upon present government programs. Not for the first time, the messenger will be upbraided for the bearing of unpopular tidings. But other agencies, both public and private, have refused to take the initiative in solving these interrelated problems that have escalated to a national crisis and are impeding our worldwide struggle against terrorism and our noble crusades for freedom and democracy in Afghanistan, Iraq and, indeed, all over the world. Under such ruses as family preservation, crypto-socialists have been bleeding the country dry of money and other essential resources, and have succeeded in turning Social Security, intended only for the truly needy at the once ripe old age of sixty-five, into what the late William Buckley deplored as a "general welfare program."

But advocates of true family preservation know that there must first be a healthy and flourishing society in which a family can take root. As noted before in this report, forty states have statutes that force the mentally ill into treatment against their will. No doubt it is a leap from compulsory therapy to the enactment of our recommended statutes that will gently and lovingly influence our seniors to partake of a permanent repose and respite from pain. And yet, surely, the chasm may be bridged with a sufficiency of media conditioning and a favorable interpretation of the Constitution, rather a simple task for the present Supreme Court, which like Baron Henry Frankenstein in the famous movie, can imbue corporations with life, de facto citizenship, and the right to participate in the political process. Said Chief Justice Charles Evans Hughes in 1907: "We are under a Constitution, but the Constitution is what judges say it is, and the judiciary is the safeguard of our liberty and of our property under the Constitution."

More recently, President Richard Nixon observed in 1974: "There is one thing solid and fundamental in politics—the law of change. What's up today is down tomorrow." And in 1984, when George H. W. Bush was a candidate for vice president, he reconsidered his position on abortion and changed from pro-choice to right-to-life. No doubt he was heeding the above- mentioned advice of President Nixon, who had rescued him from political oblivion after he lost a race for the Senate in 1970.

Sad to say, there may well be, despite our variety of programs and inducements, a remnant of selfish seniors who are disinclined to Go Ahead. Rather than give up entirely on them, we should at least educate them to shun the material pleasures made available by monthly checks from Social Security. We would encourage them to emulate the ascetic lifestyle practiced by monks and nuns of the Middle Ages. Said St. Ambrose, one of their preceptors: "Renunciation of riches is the origin and preserver of virtues."

NEWSPAPERS AND MAGAZINES

But I know newspapers. They have the first
amendment and they can tell any lie knowing
it's a lie and they're protected if the person's
famous or it's a company.
Steve Wozniak

Following the time-hallowed precedent of governments, corporations and interest groups, Sunshine Sendoffs will commission newspaper and magazine articles, and even whole books, both fiction and nonfiction, about the glory of hard work and the shame of dependency, and about the agonies of old age and the joy of participating in the Going Ahead program. In these common-sense communications, we would extol an ideology similar to that expressed in a *New York Times* column by William Safire on June 26, 2000. With his customary sagacity, this revered journalist and loyal aide to President Nixon suggested that because of increased life expectancy since the inception of Social Security, workers currently younger than fifty should not receive full benefits until retirement at seventy-two. Mr. Safire, then seventy, and never more mentally fit, judging by his political insights, added that if medical science makes great progress in curing heart disease and cancer in the years ahead, the full benefits should not begin until an even more advanced age than seventy-two.

He did not mention progress in the fight against crippling arthritis and vascular disease, but progress in those areas would presumably raise the age for full-benefits to at least eighty. After citing a report by unnamed brain scientists that a lifetime of hard work followed by a retirement devoted to fishing or loafing is "the road to degeneration and dulling of senses," Mr. Safire said that workers should reject retirement and plan second careers. Because of the current outsourcing of jobs to other countries, and the replacement of small family farms by agribusiness and mechanization, we assume that Mr. Safire, were he still alive and still disseminating his wisdom, would now advise seniors to relocate abroad for their second careers, which would further relieve the tax burden on younger Americans. The good news for seniors is that on Feb. 25, 2014, UPI reported an acute labor shortage in China, where the supply of workers had dropped to less than half of the demand.

High priority would be given to the creation of a supermarket tabloid, resembling *The National Enquirer*, that specializes in profusely illustrated articles about people who are rich and famous but also more miserable than its devoted readership of unemployed and blue-collar workers who typically have no savings but do have debts on one

or more credit cards on which they pay a monthly interest
of up to 25 percent and on which they must pay a penalty
averaging twenty dollars if they miss monthly payment by
even a day. To produce such a publication would surely
appeal to a public-spirited media entrepreneur such as
Rupert Murdoch, and he might even jump at the chance
to be interviewed about his own miseries, such as his
failure to as yet achieve what must surely be his lifetime
ambition: to own a majority of the television stations and
newspapers and magazines throughout the world, and to
be spared the burden of financial contributions to political
benefactors in the United States, the United Kingdom,
Australia and the rest of the world.

Another new magazine, targeted at the young and
edited by the consultants who run the more aggressive
campaigns of candidates for high office, would publish
articles that blamed the selfishness of seniors for all the
ills of society: decline in education, morality and family
values, and the rise in crime and violence. Seniors would
be blamed also for unemployment, inflation, ethnic unrest
and discrimination, abortion, the budget deficit, poverty
and homelessness, drug abuse, ozone depletion, climate
change, and water and air pollution, and the high cost of
living.

WEEKENDS WITH SALLY

*Even his griefs are a joy to one who remembers
all that he wrought and endured.*

Homer

A projected book, *Weekends with Sally*, will be a variation of *Tuesdays with Morrie*, the heartwarming bestseller by Mitch Albom that was made into an award-winning film with superstar Jack Lemmon. In this future classic, Cindy Ayers, a young soccer star, reminisces about her weekends over a period of six months with the ailing Sally Brewer, her soccer coach and role model back at Warren G. Harding High in a small town in the heartland of America. During one of Cindy's first weekend visits to Sally at her home, Sally tells her that she does not want her life prolonged with drugs or technology, because, as a patriotic American, she refuses to burden Social Security and Medicare a day longer than necessary.

True to her word, when her pain becomes intense and her affliction beyond a cost-efficient cure, Sally saves enough of her medications to constitute a lethal dose, and she takes it one night after viewing a World Cup soccer game in which one of her girls from Warren G. Harding High coaches a team of underdog Americans, all of them pledged to chastity, to victory over a hitherto undefeated team of steroid abusers from Brazil or Germany or Russia. Sally leaves behind a note that inspires Cindy to share her experience with others, especially with younger men and women who are concerned about the seniors in their family or circle of acquaintances.

Each of the weekend chapters begins with an inspiring quotation by a revered soccer star who is now a senior citizen and as eloquent as former baseball star Yogi Berra. If such a role model cannot be found at once and has to be developed, we would attempt to engage Roger Ailes of Fox News to teach her/him the communication skills with which he has mesmerized the nation for decades. We like to think that in the course of our association with Mr. Ailes, he will enroll in the Program and bring along fans and followers from all over the land. In the inevitable movie version of *Weekends with Sally*, Cindy might be played by Scarlett Johannsen and Sally by Academy Award winner Meryl Streep.

PAPERBACKS

All I know is what I read in the paperbacks.
                    after **Will Rogers**

We will commission a large-print paperback called *1001 Things to Be Happy About Scheduled Self-Termination.* A few suggested entries:

The dead have no tears, and forget all sorrow.

April 15 is just another wonderful day in heaven, which is a tax-free zone.

You will meet there family, friends and celebrities who have passed over.

On the other hand, heaven is so vast a place that it is easy to avoid people who have preceded you there and whom you never really liked.

Last year's clothes are never out of fashion in heaven.

Prices never rise in heaven.

On Election Day, you never have to choose between two unappealing candidates.

Ball games are never rained out in heaven.

You don't have to worry about gaining weight in heaven.

There are never any dishes to wash in heaven. Nor garbage to recycle and take out.

Heavenly supermarkets always have an ample supply of the advertised specials.

You never have to wait on line to see the latest blockbuster film in heaven.

Soda never loses its fizz in heaven, and the beer is always ice cold and with a big head.

When you have occasion to phone St. Peter or any other heavenly functionary, an angel answers at once, and he/she doesn't have a foreign accent, and you're never put on hold.

Best all, you will have an opportunity to meet George and Martha Washington in heaven. And all other past White House couples of your choice.

HAPPIER TRAILS AHEAD

Education is the result of contact. A great
people is produced by contact with great minds.
Calvin Coolidge

With Happier Trails Ahead, we will emulate successful candidates for public office, and dispatch trained, in-house educators across the country in colorful buses replete with banners and balloons. In towns large and small, our educators and local cooperating dignitaries will address citizens and answer all non-polarizing questions about Going Ahead. The words *suicide* and *sin* are to be avoided, and when used by a citizen, they must be countered with authorized terminology. Such terminology will be listed in an official manual for the aforementioned educators and dignitaries. We hope that the manual will be created by Dr. Frank Luntz, author of *Words That Work: It's Not What You Say, It's What People Hear*. For optimum effect, all discussions must, like their political prototypes, be planned ahead in the greatest detail and individualized according to local customs and political affiliations. If refreshments are served, they should be ordered from local suppliers, thus augmenting goodwill for the project. Complete cooperation is to be expected from local undertakers and affiliated business groups (vendors of sweatshirts, ice cream, etc.) who will welcome this opportunity to combine profit and patriotism.

COMPETITIONS

Through different exercises practice
has brought skill.

Manilius

Perhaps because it has the power to bring out the very best in us, there is nothing that Americans of all ages love more than a competition, not only in games and sports but also in politics and business. Americans love beauty competitions among women and athletic competitions among men. They love garden and barbecue competitions, and competitions in the sales of refrigerators and the raising of money for political candidates. In his classic study of games, *Homo Ludens* [Man the Player], Dutch historian Johan Huizinga wrote that "long before the two-party system had reduced itself to two gigantic teams whose political differences were hardly discernible to an outsider, electioneering in America had developed into a kind of national sport."

Taking advantage of this national propensity, we will encourage Going Ahead competitions among as many groups as possible: men against women, Republicans against Democrats, Red States against Blue States, baseball fans against football fans, admirers against detractors of Karl Rove and President Obama, Beatles fans against Beach Boy fans, straights against gays. Thankfully, there is an infinity of preference and interest groups in the land, and triviality has never been a deterrence to their formation and continuity over the years and decades.

The various teams will compete for the greatest and fastest enlistment of Go Aheaders, and at the moment of their self-termination, winners will exult in the knowledge of having served not only their country but also their identification group, whether it be devoted to bowling or drinking a certain brand of beer or vodka. But there will be consolation prizes for losers. As with the Miss America competition, prizes will reward sportsmanship and particular talents and skills, such as communication with household plants, collections of Barbie dolls, Hummel figures and medallions from the Franklin Mint.

MUSIC

Let us raise a somewhat loftier strain.
Virgil

We suggest that one of our first moves should be the commissioning of a musical composition that will be for Going Ahead Day the emotional equivalent of the solemn and yet jubilant "Pomp and Circumstance" march of Sir Edward Elgar. From its longtime contact with the Marches and Oratorios Division of Britain's Royal Music Society, Seneca has elicited that the most likely living composer for our "Going Ahead Day March" should be Sir Cyril Grossbeck. In recent years Sir Cyril has composed a variety of everyday and special-occasion marches for the Royal Family, and the popular British quarterly, *Better Palaces and Gardens*, reported in its June 2012 issue that the Duchess of Roseberry refused to open a flower show on the grounds of Upton Abbey unless her procession from her coach to the garden was accompanied by "Pomp and Peonies," a march composed in her honor by Sir Cyril.

We would be the first to admit that, all in all, Elgar-type music is less popular than jazz or country rock with most of our seniors as well as younger Americans, but our focus groups and polls indicate that Elgar continues to top the charts, as it were, for the few occasions that call for music that is sprightly and yet solemn and significant. In those locales where stately marches would be definitely repugnant to a substantial number of Go Aheaders and their not mourners but celebrants, we will also commission music in the styles of Willie Nelson, Glenn Miller, Guy Lombardo, and The Ink Spots. For African-Americans we may have music in the styles of Duke Ellington and Cab Calloway, and for Latinos we will have Xavier Cugat, Tito Puente, and Perez Prado. To further encourage seniors in the Latino community, we will commission an appropriate song by superstars Jennifer Lopez and Ricky Martin.

OPERATION HI THERE

Look for me in the nurseries of heaven.
Francis Thompson

Analyses of FBI crime statistics show that, year after year, the elderly are more responsive than other demographic categories to telephone sales promotions that turn out to be swindles. The bright side of this unpleasant statistic is that the elderly would be even more amenable to a telephone campaign that urged them not to spend money on nonessentials but to demonstrate their undying devotion to the country by signing up for Going Ahead. The procurement of likely subjects for our telephone program, Operation Hi There, would be the easiest part of this particular promotion. At a modest cost, or even no cost at all, their names would be obtained from such cooperative sources as HMOs with a surfeit of sickly seniors and from politicians whose older constituents (or seniles, in the vernacular of Capitol Hill) vote against them consistently because they refuse to endorse more and more entitlement programs. A word to the wise: Many an HMO and local politician would eagerly pay a finder's fee to be liberated from their undesirable seniors.

The initial targets of Operation Hi There would be seniors with medical and/or domestic problems that are beyond cost-effective amelioration in the near future. They would be phoned daily by staffers with real-life experience in interpersonal relationships with the elderly. Unusually competent at motivating the elderly are employees of nursing homes and retirement communities, and waiters and waitresses who work at the thrifty restaurants favored by seniors in Florida and Arizona. According to our preliminary research, an early recruit should very definitely be Susie Lister, a longtime waitress at Chick and Shirley's Busy Bee in Johnson City in the Sunshine State. We are informed by more than one reliable source that when patrons seek to avail themselves of the four-course, fixed-price early-bird dinner, Ms. Lister regularly warns them of the dangers of cholesterol and overweight, thus saving Chick and Shirley's Busy Bee, a subsidiary of Intercontinental Food Services of Amsterdam, LLC, the cost of serving the rich and expensive desserts—strawberry shortcake, lemon meringue pie, New York-style chocolate cheesecake—that are prime culinary enticements of the establishment. Her efforts in behalf of the distributors of Garden of Eden apple sauce and Aunt Alice's gelatin puddings have led to her being honored as waitress of the decade by *The Saturday Review of Desserts and Salads* magazine.

According to our preliminary research, the ideal leader of Operation Hi There would be Cal Maxwell Trevor, who headed the Greater All-America Life Insurance Company until he ran afoul of overly zealous officeholders in several states and was unjustly convicted of planning the campaign and phone calls that resulted in the alleged swindling of more than $100 million from people all over the country. One colleague has said of his communication skills: "If he were back in his office instead of a jail cell, he could have sold mucho shares of Japanese hotel stocks on the day after that earthquake and tsunami." Until our friends in the Justice Department are able to secure the release of Mr. Trevor from prison, he could work in his cell with the aid of the phones and computers that served him so well in the past. At wages far below those of workers outside of prison, or even of labor outsourced to China and Bangladesh, many of his fellow convicts are already hard at work for other industries, including the manufacture of shoes, textiles and furniture. In the words of former President Theodore Roosevelt, "Far and away the best prize that life offers is the chance to work hard at work worth doing. "

MEDIA MATTERS

Sound the trumpet; beat the drum...
Dryden

One or another of our task forces will contact local, state and federal law enforcement agencies and, through them, make sure that the public, especially people over sixty-five, learns every last detail about the prevalence of crimes against seniors. Some of the crimes are violent, others are white-collar swindles that deprive seniors of their homes and savings. But all these crimes could have been avoided if the victims had opted to Go Ahead when the opportunity was offered to them by a compassionate government that wished to spare them the traumas and tribulations of old age.

Just as news programs now offer segments devoted to the outstanding sports plays of the day, or the most entertaining and sexiest scandals, radio and television stations would feature the day's most heinous crime against a senior, and at the end of the week or month there should be a roundup of these atrocities, to be hosted perhaps by a real-life or cinematic figure of the eminence of Tom Hanks or the actor currently portraying Batman or James Bond. He and a panel of prominent journalists would conduct heart-breaking interviews with the victims' children and grandchildren. Bereft of an inheritance, they have been forced to abandon plans to attend college or start a small family business that might, in the great American tradition, become a multibillion dollar enterprise like Apple or Microsoft, GM or the Disney Corporation.

Whenever possible, and creative journalism should make it possible every day of the week, newspapers will have front-page headlines like the following: "Gang of 17 Sadistic Youths Held in the Fiery Death of Homeless Senior." And the victim's last words to a clergyman or paramedic might well be, "My greatest regret is that I did not die with dignity. I should have joined the Going Ahead program while I still had the chance. My final prayer is that other seniors will profit from my tragedy and visit their local Go Ahead office without delay."

TELEVISION COMMERCIALS

How sweet the truth those
blessed strains are telling.
Frederick William Faber

Our panel of motivation engineers, who have sold both popcorn and presidents to the nation, suggests that television appeals to seniors should be made during such major public events as the Academy Awards, the World Series, the Super Bowl and the Macy's Thanksgiving Day Parade. On these compelling occasions, the first one hundred seniors to enroll in the Going Ahead program will be included in a special lottery. First prize will be depiction on a postage stamp whose denomination might be the age of the winner. The ninety-nine runners-up will be awarded the Congressional Medal for Distinguished Senior Service.

Through a grass-roots organization called Citizens for a Kinder America, Sunshine Sendoffs will finance television commercials and print ads that will feature Harry and Louise, the compelling couple whose TV commercials were financed by the Health Insurance

Association in 1993, a perilous time when President Clinton and his wife, Hillary, were proposing a national health plan that would have destroyed American medicine before the advent of the next flu season. Hopefully, Goddard Claussen Porter Novelli, the public relations agency that owns the rights to the fictitious characters Harry and Louise, will allow them to appear in our own commercials. In the words of Heather von Ehrling, our media consultant, "Harry and Louise will ram home our message with the force of an appeal for big bucks by a candidate whose shtick is that he is an outsider in politics because ever since he graduated from college at the top of his class he has been busy creating quality jobs for the unemployed of all races and creeds."

If the actors who portrayed Harry and/or Louise are no longer among the living after inadequate care in a Medicaid nursing home or charity hospital, a frequent fate among freelance actors who lack the comprehensive health benefits of business executives and government officials, then look-alikes may be hired from one of many firms that over the years have been supplying look-alikes of, for example, Marilyn Monroe and Charlie Chaplin. Please see Appendix G for a rough version of a suggested sample script for the Harry-Louise commercial.

SLOGAN CONTEST

Brevity is the soul of wit.
Shakespeare

An affiliate of Seneca will suggest to the American Association of Advertising Agencies that it sponsor a slogan contest that will produce for the Program the geriatric equivalent of such confidence-generating commercial classics as "The Breakfast of Champions," "Good to the Last Drop," "From Contented Cows," "I'd Walk a Mile for a Camel," "The Pause That Refreshes," "When it Rains It Pours," "Call for Philip Morris," and "Diamonds Are Forever." The winner of the contest will be inducted into the Advertising Hall of Fame at the next annual meeting of the AAAA. We particularly admire the superb trade mark for the Lenscrafters chain of optical stores: "Are you lucky enough to need glasses?" Its creator would do well, subject to permission, to submit our suggested variant on this masterpiece of mass marketing: "Are you lucky enough to be sixty-five or over?"

Were he still alive, famed fashion designer Bill Blass would surely have submitted the superb entry, "Timing

Is Everything." This is how *The New York Times* ended his tailor-made obituary on June 13, 2002: "'The secret of living is not staying too long,' he once said. 'I have learned when to leave the party.'" Here, in the proverbial nutshell, is the philosophy that must be impressed upon seniors through a campaign of organized and cumulative information. Seneca is confident that our public and private information systems have the dedication and credibility to come through with flying colors of red, white and blue.

THE ROMANCE OF SCHEDULED
SELF-TERMINATION

Nobility is the one and only virtue.
Juvenal

To popularize the glamorous and romantic features of scheduled self-termination, Seneca will arrange with a major film studio for a new version of the popular hit of yesteryear, *Mayerling*, which depicted the ill-fated relationship of Archduke Rudolf of Austria and his inamorata Mary Vetsera. They eventually choose a scheduled self-termination rather than to live apart, even though they would be living apart in the lap of Viennese-style luxury, with boxes at the opera and at the Lippenzauer horse shows, with footmen and handmaids, fashionable clothes, and champagne with every meal unless they were in Vichy or Baden-Baden and taking there the mineral waters.

A 1936 French version starred Charles Boyer and Danielle Darrieux, and in 1968 there was an English-language version with Omar Sharif and Catherine Deneuve. But both of these productions, lauded in their day, may no longer be all that appealing to American seniors, and therefore we suggest a new version starring Clint Eastwood and Meryl Streep, mature actors who won the nation's hearts in *The Bridges of Madison County*. Also, according to our focus group, the title of the film should be changed from *Mayerling*, a resort for snobs in the faraway Austrian Alps, to *From Vegas to Eternity*. After checking in at the royal suite in the most luxurious hotel in Las Vegas, our hero and heroine would gamble recklessly, and, for their final meal, no longer afraid of cholesterol and obesity, have their fill of caviar, truffles, turtle soup, six varieties of fried potatoes with and without mushrooms and onions, assorted cheeses, filet mignon, assorted French and Austrian pastries, and chocolates.

PARADES

*However the fates may play, we march always
in the ranks of honor.*
Winston Churchill

On the weekend before the annual Go Ahead Day, seniors will be honored with the exalted and envious position of grand marshal or co-grand marshal in a parade in their hometown, whether it be Kaapahu in Hawaii or New York City. Bearing colorful banners, citizens of all ages, races, and religions will come out to line the streets. Ethnics who lack the costumes of their ancestral homeland will be provided with them for a modest price in U.S. currency by either the Costume Institute of the Smithsonian Institution or by The Costumer, which has served both professional and amateur theater groups since 1917. And every effort will be made to obtain the admiring presence of local men and women who made good in sports and entertainment.

Children will sing patriotic songs, wave flags, and hold balloons that they will eventually release according to the directions of an official balloon coordinator who has been certified by the National Association of Organizers of Political Conventions. Thanks to the sponsorship of the event by local businessmen and, hopefully, national brands such as Nike and General Foods, vendors will dispense free hot dogs and soda, free popcorn, peanuts and potato chips. Local bands and drum majorettes will demonstrate their skills. Clergy will offer their benedictions. Mayors will give speeches of supreme eloquence, and those mayors, if there be any, who feel that their eloquence is unequal to the occasion will be provided free of charge with the e-mail addresses of the talented men and women who daily write the speeches, one-liners, and off-the-cuff chitchat of the highest officials and wealthiest executives in the land.

A focus group comprised of six of the most distinguished of these experts in political communication, three Republicans and three Democrats, have agreed upon the positive impact of an introduction like the following: "Do you know something, my good friends? I think I'll forget my notes today. Because, to tell you the truth, I don't need any notes for the few words I am about to say. They are simple words that come straight from the heart. I have never been more proud of this town and its citizens of all faiths and races than I am this afternoon. In the heart and in the soul of every true American, there is a profound awareness of the concepts of challenge, opportunity, and commitment. The men and women we are honoring today have faced up to the challenge of what could and must be done without delay about the population imbalance that threatens their beloved country, the land where their fathers and mothers died, or where their fathers and mothers, if they died abroad, would have wanted to emigrate to and then die." [Give names of Go Aheaders. Give also a heartwarming anecdote about each of them. Or as many as time permits.]

After these inspiring ceremonies, which will be videotaped and included in a future documentary, hopefully by Ken Burns, award-winning creator of *The Civil War*, Go Aheaders and their families will be flown or driven by luxury bus or stretch limousine to Greener Pastures, the site of their patriotic service.

THE BIG TRAIL

*There's a long, long trail a-winding
Into the land of my dreams,
Where the nightingales are singing
And a white moon beams.*
Stoddard King

This major enrollment project will be named for *The Big Trail*, the first colossal hit in 1930 of a great patriot and immortal Western hero, John Wayne. In his dozens of films, the Duke, like Go Aheaders, was always setting out for parts unknown, but the films always had a happy ending, with the Duke in the company of a lovely and virtuous heroine who taught Sunday school and knew how to sterilize a bullet wound with whiskey but not waste a drop. The Big Trail will appeal to the millions of his fans, women as well as men, who have never experienced a great and rewarding adventure, and Going Ahead will finally give them such a, literally, once-in-a-lifetime opportunity. To introduce the project, a member of Seneca who is a longtime fan of the Duke, has suggested a TV commercial like the following, which would appear on news programs immediately after one of the periodic reports by a government agency or a cooperating think tank that Social Security and Medicare face bankruptcy in the near if not the immediate future.

While riding through Death Valley on his palomino, Academy Award winner Clint Eastwood, if he is available for this project, comes upon an oasis where he and his horse drink water from a well. There, he is visited by the spirit of his illustrious predecessor in adventure films, John Wayne. The spirit informs Eastwood of the many benefits of Going Ahead, and it orders him to form a movement that will educate other seniors to the benefits that await them at the end of The Big Trail to eternity. Eastwood agrees without hesitation, and as he resumes his ride into the sunrise, he is joined on all sides by elderly riders of both sexes, including, to be sure, African-Americans, Native Americans, Latino-Americans, and Asian-Americans.

They ride on horses and mules, in covered wagons and chuck wagons, on stage coaches and surreys. They shoot off Colts and Winchesters, sing songs, play harmonicas and banjos, and display their skills with a lariat. As they pass into the distance, a voice-over by maybe Tommy Lee Jones urges seniors to reach for their phone and dial a toll-free number. For the hard of hearing, the number is displayed on the screen in large letters. The first one hundred callers will receive, in addition to immediate induction into Going Ahead, a virtually personally inscribed photo depicting the late John Wayne as the Ringo Kid in *Stagecoach*.

GOING AHEAD DAY

Thus, thus, it is joy to pass
to the world to come.

Virgil

For a maximum of synergy, we suggest that Going Ahead Day should occur on June 14, currently celebrated as Flag Day, when every true American recalls, or should recall, the poem by Sir Walter Scott that he or she once learned in school or upon a parent's knee, and which includes the immortal lines, "Breathes there the man with soul so dead,/ Who never to himself hath said,/This is my own, my native land!"

On that glorious day, participating seniors and their loved ones from all over the country will gather in Greener Pastures, a theme park that, hopefully, will be designed by the same experts who have created theme parks for the Disney organization. In addition to the official "Going Ahead Day March" by Sir Cyril Grossbeck, a country 'n' western musician of the stature of Willie Nelson or Dolly Parton will have been commissioned to write and record a song about Going Ahead to God's Greener Pastures.

Clergymen of all faiths will be present. And so will the indispensable celebrities from the worlds of sports and entertainment.

Departers will be presented with caps and jackets with the names and logos of favorite sports teams and consumer products. Female departers will be called Golden Gals, men will be Golden Guys. A maximum of twelve caps will be presented to family and friends of the departed. There will be a parade that attempts to surpass in sound and splendor the one sponsored by R. H. Macy on Thanksgiving Day in New York City. Drum majorettes, baton twirlers, and marching bands will precede attractive and wholesome youngsters with flags and banners. The banners will identify the youth-oriented programs that, thanks to the decline of Social Security, Medicare and Medicaid have benefited from increased funding.

A highlight of the day might well be an appearance by the president of the United States and members of his extended family. And after an inspiring speech, the president and extended family will shake hands and exchange broad smiles with Go Aheaders who, to be sure, have passed a security clearance by the Department of Homeland Security. The president's speech may well be an update of the Crispian's Day speech from *Henry V* by William Shakespeare, also known to devoted fans from Maine to Hawaii as the Bard of Avon. Emulating that call for self-sacrifice by a previous head of state in a time of peril, the president will thrill Go Aheaders with the assurance that he will always regard them as brothers and sisters, and that in time to come their names will be carved forever on a roll of honor in the shadow of the Washington Monument.

After Go Aheaders have been blessed by an ecumenical synod of clergy, they will turn in their Social Security and Medicare cards to the Secretary of the Department of Progress and Opportunity, an entity that will have replaced the outmoded Department of Health and Human Services. Next, they will be offered their choice of beverages, from Kool-Aid and Diet Coke to Bud and vodka on the rocks with a twist of lemon. To all of these refreshing drinks will have been added an immortalizing dose of a painless and euphoric drug that was approved by the Food and Drug Administration and bears the coveted seal of approval of the Pharmaceutical Research and Manufacturers of America, indicating that the drug was not a cheap and illegal generic imported from Canada or China. The name of the drug will be chosen by a special committee of the National Pharmaceutical Foundation. Candidates for the special committee will be the creators of such confidence-inspiring names as Viagra, Prozac, and Claritin. Doctors and registered nurses will be at hand to prescribe and administer additional doses, if necessary.

Go Aheaders who served in the armed forces will receive a twenty-one-gun salute. Thanks to the efforts of the Congressional Caucus to Protect the Second Amendment, members in good standing of the National

Rifle Association will also be entitled to the aforementioned twenty-one-gun salute. Fireworks will be set
off as Go Aheaders retire to colorful tents above which will
proudly fly the Stars and Stripes. Southerners who wish to
fly jointly, or instead, the proud flag of the Confederacy
will, of course, be permitted to do so. And upon request,
they will be served Kentucky bourbon, a mint julep or
Southern Comfort as their final beverage. At all times,
clergy will be on hand to comfort family and friends as
they commence not the conventional grieving process
but an exultation process that has been adopted by their
faith in cooperation with the Department of Progress and
Opportunity.

As with Thanksgiving Day parades and Little
League ceremonies, it would be excellent public relations
if the expenses and promotion of Going Ahead Day
were assumed by the private sector. In that case, Seneca
would, of course, arrange with its Washington contacts
for all contributions by the private sector to be fully tax-
deductible. In accordance with the American principle of
fair play, contributing companies that have relocated to a
foreign strand and no longer pay federal or state taxes will,
whenever possible, be compensated with lucrative no-bid
contracts and/or refunds from any five years that they did
pay taxes.

TELETHONS

He who commands the home screen has command of everything.
after **Cicero**

Local and coast-to-coast telethons are a time-honored way of persuading the American people to do the right thing for fellow citizens and their country. After being conditioned by a dazzling display of dancing and singing, and then by a great entertainer with the emotional appeal of Jerry Lewis or Billy Crystal, viewers are always eager to contribute even more than they can afford to popular or obscure causes whose junk mail and e-mail they would dispose of with hardly a glance.

In a much anticipated paper that she and colleagues are preparing for a special issue of *The New England Archive of Neurology*, the preeminent journal of specialists in reactive and situational psychoses, Professor Harriet Knepper of Button Gwinnett University attributes this generous response to telethon appeals to the multimedia stimulation of the posterior part of the brain, the visual cortex. This area, in coordination with the limbic system, is also responsible to a high degree for the nurturing instinct in all primates with the possible exception of albino lemurs in the Ceriot Forest in northeast Madagascar. After studying this and other relevant papers by learned colleagues, Professor Avery F. Sawyer, our Coordinator of Geriatric Studies, believes strongly that a telethon to sign up seniors for Going Ahead must, for maximum effect, be hosted by a fellow senior who is (1) perceived by targeted viewers as "not talking out of his/her hat" but has himself/herself signed up for the program, or (2) by a pre-senior who will make a firm, on-air commitment to sign up upon reaching sixty-five, or even earlier, depending on such factors as the size of the budget deficit and the balance of trade with China.

Taking advantage of this essential information, we proceeded to conduct a series of masked polls and focus groups, the sort used daily in business and politics. Not to our surprise, they have identified the following citizens as preeminent role models for Going Ahead: Bill Clinton and George W. Bush, Michael Bloomberg and Donald Trump, Diane Sawyer and Oprah Winfrey, Ruth Bader Ginsberg and Antonin Scalia, Tom Cruise and Angelina Jolie.

Informed of these polls and their results, Professor Knepper expressed her optimism that these great and articulate Americans would appear on the telethon and then continue in their post-death process as in life to be role models for the senior citizens who had idolized them over the years and decades. Professor Knepper, born in 1970, regrets deeply that she herself, as yet, lacks the distinction to appear on the telethon with such truly accomplished and acclaimed people as Michael Bloomberg and Oprah Winfrey. In a forthcoming book, a definitive study of Sigmund Freud and the decline of the Hapsburg ethos in Vienna, she hopes to prove that Freud's frequent diagnosis of penis envy in women was really a sublimation of his own repressed case of breast envy, the etiology of which was his viewing of the famous photograph of Britain's Duke of Cramwell in a Paris brothel. The photo first appeared in the July, 1880, edition of *Liebling*, the Viennese prototype of *Playboy* magazine, first published in 1950 with a cover photo of Marilyn Monroe. Should Professor Knepper's forthcoming contribution to science be honored with the Nobel Prize and cover stories in *Time* and *Newsweek*, she would certainly wish to crown her career by appearing on our telethon and then and there pledging to Go Ahead.

SOME PERKS AND PRIVILEGES
OF GOING AHEAD

Bread and Circuses
        (Roman strategy for plebeian
        compliance with government
        policies regarding peace and war.)

Where is that good old patriotism of yesteryear,
when citizens volunteered without a moment's hesitation
for public service, and if an ultimate sacrifice were deemed
necessary by conscience or an authority figure, citizens
young and old did not hesitate to leap into the cannon's
mouth? To our great dismay, a recent poll indicates that at
the present time fully 89.3 percent of seniors interviewed
will not heed the call of their country and proceed to Go
Ahead with a light heart and brisk step. This shockingly
high number includes 84 percent of the seniors who
appeared on network and cable news channels after 9/11
and assured America and the world that they were ready,
able and willing to give their lives to protect their beloved
country from Saddam Hussein, Osama bin Laden and
terrorists both at home and abroad.

Under these sorry and disappointing circumstances, we must appeal to the baser instincts of senior citizens and offer them an assortment of perks and privileges, all more desirable than the gifts that rewarded a new bank account in the days when banks still served depositors on Main Street rather than the far more essential requirements of Wall Street. After one-on-one consultations with an elite group of motivation experts, Dr. Melvin Diamond, our director for research, offers the suggestions that follow.

*

DISCOUNTS

A penny saved is a penny earned.
Benjamin Franklin

Sunshine Sendoffs, a subsidiary of Seneca, will arrange for discounts to be extended to Go Aheaders by establishments and facilities that do not already offer them to individual seniors. The facilities may be theaters, pharmacies, restaurants and department stores, hotels and airlines, athletic stadiums, golf courses and parking lots. After debriefing our undercover agents who had investigated the practices at El Rancho Delicia, located just outside Las Vegas, we are inclined to exclude brothels from any forthcoming roster of discount establishments. With perhaps good reason, our three agents, all seniors, expressed a fear that if they had requested the 10 percent or 15 percent discount that is currently extended in many zoos and museums, they might have been offered sexual partners that gallantry and/or common courtesy would compel them to accept despite their erotogenic deficiencies.

In fairness to the management and staff of El Rancho Delicia, we are pleased to mention that Ms. Lolly Pop, former exotic dancer and currently a spokeswoman for the National Association of All-Natural and Organic Entertainment Facilities, has asserted vehemently upon many occasions that its members have never practiced any sort of discrimination and that they never will.

*

FINAL NOTES

Letters are among the most significant memorials we can leave behind.
Goethe

As they near their time to Go Ahead, men and women will surely want to send a final note of farewell in which they will also seize the opportunity to commend the program. The occasion is so important, and ghostwriting is so common these days, even at the highest level of government and business, that Go Aheaders with modest literary skills will have access to a catalogue of compositions in the styles of acclaimed communicators past and present: Abraham Lincoln, Martin Luther King Jr., Eleanor Roosevelt and Oprah Winfrey, Sarah Palin and the Reverend Billy Graham. Already in our catalogue is the following contribution by Rush Limbaugh, a longtime champion of American values who hosts the top-rated radio talk show in the country:

"If you are a true-blue, red-blooded American and not under the influence of those slimy and greedy leftist bureaucrats in Washington, this note is for you. In case you haven't noticed, we are in a war, a war for our very survival. And I'm telling it to you straight from the shoulder, like a forward pass thrown by Ronald Reagan when he was portraying the Gipper, for which role he was cheated out of an Academy Award by the lefties who controlled Hollywood at the time and still do or else they would never have handed the 2012 Academy Award for best picture to French trash called *The Artist.* Signing up for Going Ahead is by far the best thing I have ever done for my country, and I'm the guy who's been warning ever since I was still in my diapers, or so my parents tell me, about the dangers of big government and the creeping socialism that isn't just creeping anymore but racing at full speed. The Going Ahead movement is the best thing that has happened to our beloved country since the administration of Ronald Reagan, not that the two Bushes were slouches either. For one thing, Reagan knew how to handle the Mafia-style unions that were blackmailing small businesses and depriving honest, hard-working workers of decent jobs in a free market. Reagan also knew how to deregulate the banks and enable them to perform their sacred mission of transforming America into a city on a hill.

"By Going Ahead, you too, like the Gipper, can advance the march of freedom and democracy and impact future generations. But more to the point, by Going Ahead, you can avoid taxes for all time, and never again receive a parking ticket from a traffic cop who can't even tell the time of day, and you will never be told when and where you can smoke your cigar or cigarette. May God bless you, and may God bless America and the true and red-blooded patriots who fight for the principles that are essential for our current greatness and supremacy over all other nations on earth."

*

TELEVISION CAMEOS

Infinite riches in a little room.
Christopher Marlowe

One of the most coveted rewards of Going Ahead will be participation in a monthly lottery in which the grand prize will be a cameo appearance in a TV classic popular with seniors. Thanks to the computer technology that created the characters in the blockbuster film *Avatar* and the prehistoric monsters in the equally amazing

Jurassic Park, Go Aheaders will also be included in updates of popular hits of yesteryear, including *The Lucille Ball Show, Gunsmoke, The Mary Tyler Moore Show, Star Trek, Perry Mason, Seinfeld, Everyone Loves Raymond*, and *The Sopranos*. However, *Tombstone, Six Feet Under* and *Death Valley Days* will very definitely not be considered for inclusion in our repertoire of classic programs.

*

TERMINATION CARE

Old age is the harbor of all ills.
Diogenes Laertius

All our polls and focus groups tend to indicate that among the four major impediments to a quick success of Going Ahead are the immediate financial uncertainties and responsibilities of the death process when it comes. Often enough, these negative considerations are able to deter those seniors and super-seniors who would otherwise agree wholeheartedly with the oft-quoted supreme wisdom of Charles Caleb Colton: "Death is the liberator of him whom freedom cannot release, the physician of him whom medicine cannot cure, and the comforter of him whom time cannot console." True to his words, Colton, a former Anglican cleric, chose to self-terminate rather than submit to painful and uncertain surgery in 1832. We therefore propose that Medicare recipients be offered the option of buying into Termination Care, a cost-effective package of benefits that guarantees access to a dignified and self-respecting pre- and post-termination process.

As with the Medicare option of Part B, the cost of Termination Care would be deducted monthly from Social Security checks. Among the irresistible and consumer-tested benefits of Termination Care will be VIP access to a four-star funeral parlor with valet parking and to a related package of services. The services will include either a cemetery burial or a cremation, and access for up to fifty minutes to a board-certified grief counselor for the emotional closure of a group comprised of the immediate family (spouse, siblings, children, grandchildren) and up to but not exceeding four close friends. For an additional fee, other close friends as well as extended family members would be counseled as a group at a convenient Termination Care Center, which might be located at a shopping mall, multiplex cinema, or, according to season, an outdoor event such as an athletic competition or state fair. At these participating establishments, books and audiovisuals that accelerate the closure process will be available at a generous discount of a suggested 20 percent. Among the films would very definitely be our own future production, *Heaven Can't Wait,* an all-star blockbuster musical which depicts the spiritual and sensuous joys that heaven has in store for Go Aheaders.

An information sheet about Termination Care and its comprehensive benefits will be enclosed with monthly

checks from Social Security and with benefit statements
from Medicare. A typical monthly information sheet
might offer the welcome news, of no small concern to
a senior and loved ones, that Termination Care will pay
a maximum of so many inflation-indexed dollars for a
respectable coffin, but a co-payment will be required
for more elaborate receptacles and for internment in
mausoleums that are facsimiles of the resting places of
the rich and famous. Also for an additional co-payment,
either in advance by the client or posthumously by the
client's heirs, the grave will receive perpetual care in a
prestigious cemetery. A co-payment option that we hope
to make available within no more than five years after
the inception of Termination Care is internment near an
esteemed personage or celebrity, e.g., Presidents Richard
Nixon and Harry Truman, entertainers Marilyn Monroe
and Elvis Presley, sports figures Jackie Robinson and
Babe Ruth. The cost of such premium internment would
depend upon proximity to the celebrity. Should legatees
of the above celebrities object to what they might consider
a posthumous invasion of the privacy of their legator, their
lawyers and accountants will be advised to address their
complaint to the Department of Internal Revenue, and
to be prepared for an audit that will include an exhaustive
scrutiny of all possibly relevant financial documents for at
least the past fifteen years.

Go Aheaders who prefer cremation will receive a free
video from a lifestyle guru of the stature of Martha Stewart

if not from Ms. Stewart herself. Her expertise with shapes and decorations will allow seniors to Go Ahead with the confidence that they have selected the absolutely correct urn for their earthly remains. As we learn from a recent trade show of the funeral industry at the Javits Center in New York City, urns and their display have become an increasingly popular conversation piece in such pacesetting communities as the Hamptons on Long Island, K Street in Washington, and Malibu in California. We expect that Ms. Stewart, in her video, will offer the latest authoritative advice about the aesthetic relationship of urns to such other household components as rugs and carpets, drapes, period and contemporary furniture, entertainment units, uniforms of maids and other indoor servants, and even breed and color of pets.

*

PETS AND PLANTS

The more people I see, the more I admire my dogs.
Count D'Orsay

Thanks to their Termination Care coverage, seniors who are reluctant to Go Ahead because of responsibilities to pets and plants will no longer have a valid reason to delay an early participation in the program. In fact, being assured of daily scientific feeding and both verbal and tactile communication rather than the unreliable attention of a feeble senior who cannot even care for herself/himself properly, pets and plants will in most cases—fully 88 percent, according to Belle Conrad, bestselling author of *I Speak to My Daisies, and They Answer Me!*—fare better than ever after their departure. Within hours of the Going Ahead of a beloved master or mistress, the American Association for the Preservation of Household Fauna and Flora, having employed its computerized matching system, will see to it that pets and plants are placed in new homes that will closely resemble their former ones, and may even be an improvement! For a slight additional fee, plants may be relocated to a national park selected by a horticulturist affiliated with the world-famous Atlanta Botanical Garden.

Further, seniors without kin or close friends will be able to rest assured that their cars and guns, their precious Bibles and priceless official photos of the Bush or Clinton families, their golf clubs and fishing rods, computers and other valued possessions will be properly cared for by kindred spirits. As was the custom in other times and places, seniors may, of course, choose to have their valuables buried with them, and commodious coffins will be available for this purpose. Also available, for an additional small fee, will be the services of VIP Voyage, the team of experts who pack the clothing and other necessities of the rich and famous when they depart for an extended cruise.

*

SEX

*What though strength fails... In mighty
enterprises, it is enough to have had the
determination.*
Sextus Aurelius Propertius

A certain sensitive question has been raised informally
by an officer of Seneca, and it would be remiss if we did
not discuss it at this point. On the eve of their Going
Ahead, should seniors still interested in interpersonal sex
be rewarded with a bonus of a physical encounter with an
attractive partner? And if the answer is in the affirmative,
should sexually inclined males be offered Viagra or Cialis
and females be offered Potomac Passion, Beltway Bliss,
Soho Siren, or one of the other stimulants that are reputed
to be popular in Washington, New York City, and other
areas where recreational sex is a fashionable pursuit akin
to brewing coffee beans from a particular hillside on a
remote island in the Pacific? And what if the preferred
sexual partner is of the same sex as the Go Ahead, which
many elected and appointed government officials, in their
devotion to sound family values, deplore as an unnatural
relationship for constituents even when they themselves
and family members secretly or overtly engage in such
relationships?

A grateful nation should certainly wish to offer a

maximum of rewards to Go Aheaders, but after a double-blind experiment conducted on our behalf by the Institute of Advanced Geriatric Sexual Studies at Princeton, New Jersey, we have concluded that sexual gratification on the eve of their Going Ahead may well cause seniors to postpone or even cancel entirely their scheduled departures. Having researched the history of some of the more traditional voluntary commitments, such as promises to fund a charity or endow a college, Jonathan Dwayne Warricker, law professor at Wiggley University, believes that when a senior makes a written commitment to Go Ahead, this entirely voluntary action is tantamount to joining the armed forces, or the signing of a contract to purchase a good or service, and that the senior's violation of it must be punished by the usual fine, imprisonment, or even both, depending upon the circumstances and heinousness of the violation.

Because, according to a poll conducted by I Hear America Talking, the fining and/or incarceration of their aged parents and grandparents will not prove popular among the general public, Seneca takes a firm position that the Senior Citizen Growth and Opportunity Act should refrain from encouraging any and all sorts of sexual activity for Go Aheaders. If the matter of sex comes up at all, Go Aheaders may be informed that it is one of the pleasures that await them in heaven. This explanation should satisfy people with the IQ to wish to participate in the program at all, according to Francine O. Burstine, professor of advanced sexual dynamics at the aforementioned Institute of Advanced Geriatric Sexual Studies.

*

FINANCIAL INCENTIVES

If you should put a little on a little, and should do this often, soon this too would become big.
Hesiod

Thirty days before their departure, seniors who avail themselves of the golden and literally once-in-a-lifetime opportunity to participate in Going Ahead will receive a tax-free payment not to exceed the sum of two thousand dollars, the exact amount depending on marital status and monthly benefit check from Social Security. If they themselves do not spend the entire sum, the balance may be bequeathed to heirs or to a favorite cause. Under no circumstances may any part of the bequest be donated, either directly or indirectly, to an individual or group that advocates policies detrimental to America and its values. To further prevent money from reaching any enemies of freedom, a list of groups favored and forbidden by the federal government will be included with the check. State and local governments may add further restrictions.

*

WHO'S WHO IN THE HEREAFTER

He lives in fame that died in virtue's cause.
Shakespeare

Among the more enticing rewards of Going Ahead will surely be inclusion in an annual directory to be called *Who's Who in the Hereafter.* Alone or with the assistance of family and friends, the Go Aheader can write his/her own entry in two hundred words or fewer. Or, for a modest fee, Go Aheaders may prefer to have an entry composed by a computer program that will be created according to the specifications of a prize-winning communicator. Among the world-class communicators whom we hope to engage for the directory are past and current White House counselors and press chiefs, editorial page editors of *The Wall Street Journal* and *The New York Times*, writers of productive advertisements for products and services, writers of the annual reports of corporations, mutual funds and hedge funds. And, last but not least, creators of TV ads for political candidates. As a public service, one of these superb communicators, whose modesty compels anonymity at this time, has been kind enough to offer a sample of her skills in behalf of a Republican Go Aheader. But she gives assurances that she would do no less for a Democrat.

Charles (Chuck) Groppheim (1940-2014)

Former President George W. Bush has often confided to friends who shared his dreams for America that he was thinking of good old Chuck Groppheim when he coined the phrase "compassionate conservative." Over the years, since their first meeting atop the Statue of Liberty on July 4, 1995, Chuck, a soybean farmer from Iowa, had stressed the necessity for smaller government, bigger farm subsidies, low taxes, and the overwhelming importance of a space program that would provide a shield against missiles from rogue states on our own planet or from distant galaxies.

There was nothing fancy about Chuck, who always preferred domestic to imported beer, Frank Sinatra to grand opera, Norman Rockwell to Pablo Picasso, and American cheese to smelly cheeses from countries where presidents had mistresses as well as wives. Up in heaven, Chuck is more proud than ever of his gorgeous wife, Jean, and his daughters Helen and Betty and their families, and of the fact that he never in his whole life voted for anyone but a Republican. His favorite quotation was and still is one by President Ronald Reagan: "We're the party that wants to see an America in which people can still get rich."

*

WIT AND WISDOM FROM THE HEREAFTER

What is truth? said jesting Pilate, and would
not stay for an answer.
Francis Bacon

What senior has not had a clever thought or two about things that happen down here on earth or may happen up above in heaven? Once they are in heaven, as they surely will be after their supreme act of valor for their country, the thoughts of Gone Aheaders will, with the aid of cooperating mediums and telepathists, be included in an annual book to be called *Wit and Wisdom from the Hereafter*. In addition, we will make every effort to include their thoughts in one or more volumes of the *Chicken Soup* series, and in one of the following ever-popular features in *Reader's Digest*: "Personal Glimpses," "Laughter," "Points to Ponder," and "Notes from All Over."

Here is a wonderful opportunity for all seniors, regardless of their IQ, academic credentials, or skills in grammar and punctuation, to be included in the same publication with such previously deceased literary greats as Ralph Waldo Emerson, James Fenimore Cooper, Henry Wadsworth Longfellow, Ayn Rand, William F. Buckley Jr., John Greenleaf Whittier, Mark Twain, and educator Horace Mann, who as long ago as 1859, and perhaps with a prevision and endorsement of our own Going Ahead

145

program, said in a commencement address at Antioch College: "Be ashamed to die until you have won some victory for mankind."

*

OBITUARIES

A great man can come from a hut.
Seneca

The Senior Citizen Growth and Opportunity Act will establish a commission that encourages hometown newspapers to publish obituaries of Go Aheaders. Hopefully, the commission will include such time-tested masters of persuasion as former Secretary of State James A. Baker 3rd and former President Bill Clinton. Members of the commission will even contact such elite newspapers as *The New York Times* and *The Washington Post*, which usually ignore the socially obscure unless they committed a major crime or were ever involved in a major scandal, whether financial, political, or sexual. To insure the cooperation of newspaper editors and publishers, the commission will establish links with the local leaders and businessmen upon whom their publication depends for advertising revenue, parking facilities, favorable tax assessments, leniency for narcotics violations, and speeding tickets incurred by editors, publishers and selected employees to a maximum of twelve.

If the departed accomplished little or nothing of note, journalistically speaking, then his/her modesty and devotion to family, garden, and pets will be praised as being far from the ordinary. On their evening news programs, networks and cable outlets will be asked to schedule a weekly segment to be called, perhaps, "Gone, but Never to Be Forgotten." Further, in an emulation of the *Biography Channel*, each and every Go Aheader will be remembered on an *Obit Channel* that will have been established on cable television. Once in full swing, the *Obit Channel* should attract more viewers and advertisers than the specialty channels that are currently devoted to the promotion and sale of motivation programs, cosmetics and jewelry, home and health products, and exercise equipment. A popular feature of the *Obit Channel* will be that Go Aheaders and/or designated representatives can choose in advance the background music to be played during their individualized segment. We hope to secure permission to use the following singers and their most appropriate hits:

Doris Day	"Sentimental Journey"
Peggy Lee	"We'll Meet Again"
Don Cherry	"I'll Be Around"
Frank Sinatra	"My Heart Stood Still"
Eddie Fisher	"Oh, My Papa"
Al Martino	"My Wish Came True"

Petula Clark	"Kiss Me Goodbye"
Barbra Streisand	"The Way We Were"
The Beatles	"Magical Mystery Tour"
Yanni	"Port of Mystery"
Roy Rogers	"Happy Trails Ahead"
Gene Autry	"Back in the Saddle Again"
Willie Nelson	"On the Road Again"

*

LAST VIDEOS

A house of dreams untold
That looks out over the whispering treetops
And faces the setting sun.
Edward MacDowell

On the weekend before the scheduled departure of Go Aheaders for Greener Pastures, the heavenly locale of their unique and inimitable service to the country, Sunshine Sendoffs will arrange with Netflix or other providers for Go Aheaders to receive not only three free movies, whether new releases or golden oldies, but also three free bags of popcorn and three free cans of their favorite soft drink. However, X-rated films may not be requested by seniors on their last night. In defense of this exclusion, which at first glance may seem to violate the First Amendment, a senior fellow on Seneca's panel of video advisers likes to quote Jeremiah Brown Howell (1772-1822), who served in the Senate early in the nation's history: "We are saved from nothing if we are not saved from sin. Little sins are pioneers of hell."

Frederick Peabody, our chairman emeritus, offers the excellent suggestion that Go Aheaders view videos of the following films: *Gladiator, Saving Private Ryan, Patton, High Noon, Shane, Dark Victory, The Magnificent Seven* and *Titanic*. All of these prize-winning classics depict and glorify commendable conduct when faced with the inevitable.

*

TERMINAL ATTIRE

Costly thy habit, as thy purse can buy,
But not express'd in fancy; rich, not gaudy;
For the apparel oft proclaims the man
and the maid.

Shakespeare
(gender-neutral update)

Even more important than first impressions in life are last impressions in death, and Go Aheaders must be made aware of this fact. A poor first impression may be corrected eventually, but a bad last impression will be remembered forever. Therefore, the good news is that, if they so wish, Go Aheaders will be provided free of charge with makeup and a choice of wigs for viewing of their earthly remains. They will also receive free cleaning for their burial clothes. According to most Judeo-Christian theologians of our own day, it is unlikely that the body as well as the soul is immortal, but folk wisdom and some of the great theologians of the past believed otherwise, and so why should Go Aheaders take a chance on looking less than their best and most attractive when they reach the other side? In any case, whatever fate awaits them, Go Aheaders will be pleased to know that their loved ones will have a final chance to see them in all their cosmetic and sartorial glory.

Because nothing can be too bizarre and yet popular for a month or even a season in the world of fashion, one of our subsidiaries will arrange for a team of world-class couturiers, hopefully the ones who design gowns for the Oscar awards, to design also unisexual shrouds and coffin garments of various colors and textiles. The shrouds and garments will be free, because, hopefully, after a fashion show of these creations, a mature male and female movie star of the luster of Meryl Streep and Alec Baldwin will become models and spokespersons for Death and Transfiguration, a chain of unisex boutiques that may one day become as popular and profitable as Victoria's Secret and The Gap.

*

ACTIVITIES GALORE!

Mirth, admit me of thy crew,
To live with her, and live with thee,
In reproved pleasures free.
Milton

Go Aheaders will be rewarded with a card entitling them and a guest to reduced prices or even free admittance to the Disney parks, and to rodeos and state fairs, poker tournaments, beauty contests, museums, plays, operas, ballet and sports events, and zoos and botanic gardens. When they attend an aquarium with performing seals and dolphins, they will be honored by being permitted to throw fish to the dolphins, to hold hoops for them to jump through, and to interact with them in all other ways that are agreeable to local chapters of the Humane Society and the American Society for the Prevention of Cruelty to Animals. Aquariums are often hazardous underfoot, especially for seniors. And unforeseen injuries may also occur at rodeos and even at an opera, where a tenor can be more adept at hitting a high C than hitting his onstage target with a lance, thereby piercing a Go Aheader in a front row. Therefore, accident insurance will be made available at a reduced price to Go Aheaders and up to four members of his/her group.

*

ON WINGS OF SONG

When I am dead, my dearest,
Sing no sad songs for me.
Christina G. Rossetti

Thanks to the wonderful world of computers and to generous contributions toward the establishment of a National Endowment for the Senior Arts, we have every hope of persuading superstar musician Elton John to do for Go Aheaders what he did for Marilyn Monroe and Princess Diana, and write a virtually individualized song in their memory. If Elton John does not turn them on, Go Aheaders may choose to be memorialized instead by Stephen Sondheim, Paul McCartney, Andrew Lloyd Weber, or by Lady Gaga for seniors in their second childhood, or any other popular composer or lyricist who is cooperating with the program, and it is hard to believe that any will shirk their responsibility.

Pending final approval by their estates or the music repositories of the Library of Congress, the British Museum, and the Vienna Academy of Music, songs will also be available in the styles of Scott Joplin, Victor Herbert, Rodgers and Hammerstein, Jerome Kern, Irving Berlin, Duke Ellington, Gilbert and Sullivan, Noel Coward, Franz Schubert, Johannes Brahms, and Wolfgang Amadeus Mozart.

*

PRESIDENTIAL CONVENTIONS

Every public office, small or great, is held in trust for your fellow-citizens.
Grover Cleveland

Though they lack the clout and/or the financial generosity of official delegates, duly certified Go Aheaders will be admitted to the convention of their choice in the year of a presidential election. There they will be extended the great honor of an upholstered but back-row seat in their state delegation. And they will be further honored with a flag, banner, and distinctive badge. According to their sex and the past sexual scandals of their governor, they will also receive from him/her either a handshake or a kiss and heartfelt hug.

Also at the convention, for a contribution of no more than five thousand dollars, payable in advance, a Go Aheader's name will be invoked in a speech by a candidate. The candidate will recall what a great inspiration the Go Aheader has always been to him, and the candidate may even relate a heartwarming anecdote about the Go Aheader. The results of an informal poll indicate that Peggy Noonan, speechwriter for President Reagan, should be engaged to rewrite and, if necessary, to create the anecdotes.

Should the preferred presidential candidate be elected

to office, the Go Aheader and a spouse or significant other will be invited to an inaugural ball for a modest donation of at least twenty-five thousand dollars. This is, of course, a fraction of the suggested voluntary contribution of non-Go Aheaders, who must contribute up to at least ten times as much, both directly or indirectly. Go Aheaders and spouses are expected to provide their own evening attire and limousines to the assigned banquet hall. Go Aheaders living on a fixed income may share a limousine if the model and its length and luster are acceptable to the official inauguration committee. Also, they must pledge not to try to bond at the ball or elsewhere in Washington with busy CEOs, lobbyists and government officials who, as much as they would like to, have no time to spend with moribund strangers without commercial, social or political value to them.

Go Aheaders with no particular interest in politics, or with a disability that would be adversely affected by the nonstop handshaking and backslapping of a political convention, will be admitted instead to a trade show or art exhibition of their choice. Preferably, the trade show will be devoted to products that are candidates for a Good Housekeeping seal of approval or could be advertised with pride in family magazines or on radio and television stations that are supervised by the Federal Communications Commission. Go Aheaders will be assured that all the art exhibitions have been cleared for X-rated material by a panel headed by such a true-and-tried advocate of cultural cleanliness as former Mayor Rudy Giuliani of New York City. Whether they opt for the political convention, trade show, or art exhibit, Go Aheaders will receive a travel voucher of up to but not exceeding two hundred dollars.

*

CIGARS

And a woman is only a woman, but a good cigar is a smoke.
Rudyard Kipling

Despite the federal government's ban on the import of Cuban cigars ever since the violent revolution of communist dictator Fidel Castro in 1959, it is common knowledge that they have long been available to VIPs in all walks of life, whether at country clubs, board meetings on Wall Street, or political fundraisers in the Beltway. Said President Eisenhower toward the end of his decades of public service, "We have never stopped sin by passing laws; and in the same way, we are not going to take a great moral ideal and achieve it merely by law."

From the first day of the month after their signing up for the program until their great day of service to the nation, Go Aheaders who have never achieved the status of VIP may purchase monthly for a fair-market price a maximum of five Cuban cigars of any brand or size. Nonsmokers may purchase the five cigars and either give them away or sell them, but only to members of their nuclear family or to a friend who has sworn before a county clerk or notary public to have been a friend for at least twelve months. Both family members and friends must swear also that they have never in any way supported the Marxist policies of Cuban dictator Fidel Castro and his successors. Go Aheaders who have always lived on a modest income and could never afford a Cuban cigar, will receive gratis an informative booklet that includes tips on the treatment of nausea and smoke inhalation written by a top VIP and true connoisseur of cigars, perhaps superstar Jack Nicholson.

*

LIQUOR AND HAPPY HOURS

How oft when men are at the point of death
Have they been merry.
Shakespeare

In some of the fifty states, the law requires liquor stores to close for all or part of Sunday. However, for the two Sundays prior to Departure Day, Go Aheaders may purchase up to two bottles of any alcoholic beverage at a designated liquor store that will be no more than forty-five miles away from their community. For Go Aheaders who prefer to drink in bars and restaurants, the Sunday hours at their favorite establishment will begin two hours earlier than the hitherto legal hours. Also for Go Aheaders at bars and restaurants, the Happy Hour on all days of the week will begin two hours earlier than for younger patrons.

Seniors who have not yet committed themselves to Going Ahead will be severely punished if they misrepresent their status and apply at an early hour for refreshments intended solely for drinkers dedicated to their country as well as to their personal pleasure.

*

FLYING SAUCERS

Time is flying never to return.
Virgil

Breathes there a well-informed citizen who has not expressed a wish to learn the truth about flying saucers? Go Aheaders and spouses will be invited to a top secret military base in the Arizona desert for a special seminar on one of the great mysteries of all time: Does life as we know it in America, especially barbeques and beauty contests, exist elsewhere in the universe, and has Earth been visited by extraterrestrials in flying saucers or other vehicles that more resemble our own civilian and military aircraft? If life does exist on Mars, what sort of body and mind do its inhabitants have? Do they, like average Americans, partake of the benefits of a great and unique civilization, and enjoy baseball and cheeseburgers, gambling casinos in

Las Vegas and trips to the shopping mall? Such questions have enthralled seniors ever since they were exposed to the exploits of Buck Rogers and Flash Gordon in their youth, and now they, and only they, will be getting the answers.

Among the panel of experts, in addition to scientists from around the world, and perhaps a mystery guest from outer space, we hope to have William Shattner and Leonard Nemoy, stars of the original *Star Trek* series, and Harrison Ford and James Earl Jones of the *Star Wars* movies. Every effort will be made to persuade the four stars, all seniors, to sign up for Going Ahead and to autograph the comic books and collectibles of fans who have preserved them over the years and decades.

*

FOR CONSTANT READERS

*Dreams, books, are each a world; and books,
we know,
Are a substantial world, both pure and good.*
Wordsworth

Upon signing up with the Go Ahead program, fans of Stephen King, Danielle Steel, John Grisham, and Sue Grafton and other popular authors will receive free advance copies of their latest novels. The books, each with a personalized inscription, are destined to become beloved family heirlooms, and in time to come will be evaluated at one thousand dollars or more, according to Research Director Melvin Diamond, who has strong contacts with the popular PBS television program *Antiques Road Show.* We are confident that, in his inscriptions, Stephen King will assure fans that the horrors in his novels do not await them in the hereafter. On the contrary, he will see fit to quote the following positive thought by his equally famous colleague, William Shakespeare, "Heaven, the treasury of everlasting joy."

And we are equally confident that romance novelist Danielle Steel will assure her fans that they can expect there true and everlasting love, not only in the spiritual sense but perhaps also in the physical. Sue Grafton, of course, will convince them that *H* is for *heaven,* not for *hell.* As for the fans of Grisham, they will be assured of the eventual and eternal triumph of relatively poor but honest lawyers over wealthy colleagues who work for greedy corporations.

*

GARDEN OF MEMORY

God Almighty first planted a garden.
Francis Bacon

A rose of award-winning beauty will be cultivated and named for Go Aheaders in the National Garden of Memory, to be established inside or adjacent to Arlington

National Cemetery. Go Aheaders who are allergic to or do not particularly care for roses may select any other flower except orchids, which would require special permission from the Secretary of Agriculture. Macho men who would disdain association with a flower may request the substitution of a fruit or vegetable. Chick peas, lima beans and kidney beans will be perfectly in accord with the mission statement of the National Garden of Memory.

*

ESTATE PLANNING

What gift has Providence bestowed on man
that is so dear to him as his children?
Cicero

Go Aheaders who wish to provide for family but lack confidence in their own financial judgment will have a free eight minute telephone consultation with a licensed analyst associated with a world-class investment company of the stature of Morgan Stanley Chase. Profiting from the track record through bull and bear markets of this financial guru who survived the Great Recession and afterwards received a generous bonus, Go Aheaders will learn the ten investment tips and twelve tax loopholes that are guaranteed to enhance their estates and up-value the portfolios of their heirs by fully 12.5 percent, despite market fluctuations that may be bankrupting other investors.

*

PHOTO OPPORTUNITY

*If you can't be great yourself, you can achieve a
virtual greatness by being photographed with
someone who is.*
Eric Roy

Go Aheaders will be able to enjoy photo and/or
handshaking opportunities with up to three past and
present celebrities—even presidents! Go Aheaders must
provide their own cameras and transportation to the site
of the photo opportunity. Should the site be a tennis
court or golf course at a country club, a locale favored
by celebrities, Go Aheaders must arrange for their own
guest pass and must pay the standard admittance fee,
which usually does not include parking privileges and
gratuities. Sometimes but not always, according to the
expenditure philosophy of the celebrity, Go Aheaders will
be expected to buy at least two rounds of drinks for their
chosen celebrity and his/her guests at the country club.
Peanuts and chips are usually served free with the drinks,
but Go Aheaders should be forewarned that celebrities
may be aficionados of the newer and costly snacks from
such upscale haunts as Montauk and Monte Carlo.

Because political figures are trained to display their
friendliness with a vigorous handshake and/or backslap,
Go Aheaders who suffer from arthritis or bone or joint

disorders will be advised to take protective measures although, of course, any medical bills will be paid by Medicare and a supplemental insurer such as AARP. On the other hand, Go Aheaders who hate big government and have contracted with a private insurer may experience difficulty in receiving treatment for injuries that were triggered by a preexistent condition from decades ago. Nevertheless, they should rejoice in the fact that a for-profit enterprise is competing with Medicare and Obamacare, and that, thanks to relentless lobbying and financial contributions to key government officials, his insurer may replace them eventually.

*

RESTROOM FACILITIES

One touch of nature makes the whole world kin.
Shakespeare

Through its friends at all levels of government and their relevant agencies, Sunshine Sendoffs will strive to obtain for Go Aheaders an ID card that entitles them to be advanced at once to the head of the restroom queue at ballgames, in theaters, and in other public places with the exception of rock and folk music concerts starring left-wing entertainers. This restroom privilege may be objectionable to many libertarians and strict egalitarians, but we would like to cite in its defense the universally accepted practice of priority boarding for pregnant women and the physically handicapped on commercial airlines, and for priority treatment of public officials and other VIPs in the admitting offices and emergency rooms of hospitals. We would hate to think that the vast majority of pre-seniors, possessed of stronger bladders and other relevant organs, will want to deny this small privilege to seniors who will soon be making the supreme sacrifice for them.

If there be two or more Go Aheaders who are simultaneously heeding nature's call between acts at a dramatic or musical presentation, as may well be the case on Wednesday and weekend matinees, they will receive preference in order of age and severity of physical or psychosomatic problems, of which there are sure to be several. Both of these factors—age and special problems—will be noted on the cards that identify them as members in good standing of the Go Ahead community. For quick identification in a theatrical environment, the cards of seniors with severe and unusual problems will bear the Greek mask for tragedy. To avoid arguments among seniors that may prove more compelling to other theater patrons than the dramatic offering in the auditorium, Go Aheaders will be advised to carry also medical reports from their geriatricians, psychotherapists, urologists and gastrointestinal specialists.

*

PARKING PRIVILEGES

But at my back I always hear
Time's winged chariot hurrying near;
And yonder all before us lie
Deserts of vast eternity.
Andrew Marvell

For up to three months prior to their day of departure, Go Aheaders with driving licenses in good order may park day and night, seven days a week, on streets and in areas hitherto forbidden to them and other demographic categories unless they enjoyed the current special privileges of doctors and clergy on call, and of those judges and other government officials who believe that their familiarity with the law entitles them to flout it with immunity upon occasion.

Further, Go Aheaders will no longer be required to put coins into public parking meters, even at peak hours. Restaurants that currently offer a period of free parking to patrons will be asked to extend the courtesy for additional hours but to no more than eight. Hotels that currently charge for parking and valet parking will be asked to waive that expenditure for Go Aheaders. Tipping will remain at the discretion of car owners although garage employees will be encouraged to refuse them.

*

PRESIDENTIAL PARDONS

I know in my heart that man is good. That
what is right will always eventually triumph.
And there's purpose and worth to each and
every life.
Ronald Reagan

If they volunteer to Go Ahead at the next official
date, seniors who were once convicted of a misdemeanor
or felony by a jury of their peers and duly punished
according to law will be released from prison no later than
two business days after the approval of their applications.
If they were fined as well as or instead of being imprisoned,
the complete sum will be returned, and with the same rate
of interest, if any, that is currently being paid by the bank
nearest their last official residence prior to incarceration.
Homeless convicts who were fined will receive a rate of
interest to be determined by the Chairman of the Federal
Reserve Board in consultation with the Secretary of the
Treasury and the American Bankers Association.

As a special bonus, Go Aheaders who persuade fellow
inmates to follow their patriotic example will, within
thirty days prior to their self-termination, also have their
fingerprints and all criminal records removed from the files
of all local, state and federal law enforcement agencies.
This will be a priceless legacy for children who run for

public office or expect appointment to the judiciary or to membership in the president's cabinet. In a time when politics has never been more savage, and the spoils of offices more lucrative, the children will now be able to claim with pride and deniability that they learned family and social values at the knee of a parental mentor with a spotless record.

Also, as a token of appreciation to seniors who were once associated with the political and/or business machinations of Bill and Hillary Clinton but who now consent to Go Ahead at the next official date, we hope to arrange for former Special Prosecutor Kenneth Starr and a committee of elite Republicans to offer a handsome certificate attesting to their patriotism, honesty, character, and total dedication to American values. Needless to say, a similar offer will be extended to Republicans who were criminally involved in the Watergate and Iran-Contra indiscretions of the Nixon and Reagan administrations.

*

LAST MEALS

Better is a dinner of herbs where love is, than a stalled ox and trouble therewith.
Psalms 15:17

On the day before their departure for Greener Pastures, Go Aheaders will be treated to a gala dinner—or, if they prefer, breakfast, brunch, lunch, or barbeque—either at home or in a restaurant with a rating of up to two stars. Toward the end of their meal at the restaurant, and with great ceremony that will surely attract and inspire other senior patrons, the mâitre d' will present them with an elaborate cake topped with the symbol of the Going Ahead program, which may be a harp whose strings have been replaced with an American flag. As the cake is being cut, all present will sing "For He (or She)'s a Jolly Good Patriot." At the restaurant, the mâitre d' and an attractive hostess will distribute applications for Going Ahead to other diners.

Also, if our hopes are realized, Go Aheaders can, for a modest fee of about five hundred dollars, not including gratuity and restaurant or tavern taxes in their state or city, be a dinner guest of a famous or admired personage from our contemplated panel of affiliated hosts and hostesses. They will be women and men from all walks of life, and of the towering stature or celebrity of Dick Cheney, Bill Clinton, Oprah Winfrey, Rudy Giuliani, Diane Sawyer, Newt Gingrich, Ann Coulter, Henry Kissinger and Sarah Palin. Wherever they choose to enjoy this very special meal, vegetarians will be assured of organic produce from nearby farms. Abstainers from alcohol will be offered juices and ciders that have been personally selected by a top official of Alcoholics Anonymous.

Hy Brett

*

FRANKLIN MINT

O Attic Shape! Fair attitude.
Keats

Aware of their great popularity with cultured and discriminating seniors, we hope to arrange with the Franklin Mint, manufacturers of world-famous collectibles, for a modestly priced limited-edition coin, figurine, or dish with the likeness of a Go Aheader. Like all other products of the Franklin Mint, this very special objet d'art will surely became a revered classic within months of its creation by a world-class artist whose other works, if they do not already do so, may one day draw record crowds at the Louvre Museum in Paris and the Metropolitan Museum of Art in New York City.

We do not expect an extra charge for a dual portrait with a spouse or a pet unless it is a fish in a tank, but a dual portrait with the likeness of a revered statesman such as former Presidents George H. W. Bush or President Harry S. Truman will cost a thousand dollars and may well require an FBI security clearance of the Go Aheader and his/her family and friends and past and present business associates. Depending upon the extension and depth of the investigation, and the Go Aheader's past or present residence in such dubious environments as Brooklyn and Greenwich Village, such clearance may well take up to a year and cost at least an additional five thousand dollars.

*

CONCERT BY THE THREE GO AHEADERS

I have a song to sing, O! Sing me your song, O!
W. S. Gilbert

On a Saturday night about a week before Going Ahead Day, a concert by The Three Go Aheaders will be offered at the Kennedy Center in Washington. Their program of mostly operatic arias will have been selected in a nationwide ballot of fellow Go Aheaders. At least three months before the concert, officers of a new organization, the National Endowment for the Senior Arts, will conduct nationwide auditions for the performers. Knowledge of Italian, German, French and Russian will be helpful but not essential, thus complying with laws against discrimination.

Also in accordance with anti-discrimination laws, the National Endowment for the Senior Arts will commission maestro James Levine and superstar soprano Renee Fleming to audition Go Aheaders for the following vocal groups: The Three Go Ahead Sopranos, The Three Go Ahead Mezzos, The Three Go Ahead Tenors, The Three Go Ahead Coloraturas, The Three Go Ahead Baritones,

The Three Go Ahead Bassos, and The Three Go Ahead Countertenors.

*

EULOGIES

It is sweet and seemly to die for one's country.
(A Roman creed, attributed to Horace,
and often inscribed on tombstones)

After the usual heartfelt and totally sincere eulogies by a clergyman and family and friends, whether at a funeral parlor or gravesite, Go Aheaders will be further honored by a personalized, five-minute videotaped eulogy by their choice of eloquent celebrities, including Meryl Streep and Tom Hanks, Rush Limbaugh, Reverends Al Sharpton and Pat Robertson, former Presidents Clinton and Bush. Because of the previous commitments and fully booked speaking tours of these busy people, which often result in sore throats and laryngitis, Go Aheaders will be encouraged not to delay in submitting the necessary information about their lives and virtues and deeds, and their favorite foods, drinks, sports heroes and teams, recipes, and junk foods, and favorite entertainers and athletes, clergymen, celebrities, political parties, and pets and political leaders.

*

CALENDARS

Lives of great men all remind us
We can make our lives sublime,
And, departing, leave behind us
Footprints in the sands of time...
Longfellow

One of our subsidiaries, Tempus Fugit, would arrange for the distribution to Go Aheaders and to potential Go Aheaders of a free calendar with a different monthly picture and quotation about the pains of old age and the joys of self-termination and immortality. The calendar would also be available at supermarket racks devoted to sensational tabloids and romance novels. And we would arrange with cooperating post offices and with Yahoo, Google and Microsoft Live for the calendar to arrive in the mail and/or email on the same day as such unwelcome communications as utility and credit-card bills, and with heartbreaking monetary appeals from political candidates who are millionaires. And from charities that claim to care for endangered species they never knew existed, and with monthly and quarterly reports from mutual funds that have been underperforming. And with notices from former employers that, having fulfilled their legal commitments to management and directors regarding bonuses and other financial obligations, they have now declared bankruptcy and are no longer legally bound to provide monthly health benefits and pension checks to retirees although their contribution to the company will always be remembered and appreciated.

To induce recipients to display their calendar in a prominent place where its message will reach and inspire visiting seniors, the lovely, full-color illustrations will be by Norman Rockwell and Thomas Kinkade, great American painters whose depictions of the heartland will, according to the head of our team of motivation engineers, "subliminally compel senior viewers to neutralize negative associations regarding the death process and substitute the positive feelings of their first encounter with the typical subject of a painting by Rockwell and Kinkade." Early pictures will include a visit to an ice cream parlor on Main Street, a chili lunch on a porch or backyard, a Sabbath dinner in a cottage down a country road. The expected result of the calendar exposure will be a deep compulsion for seniors—in fact, upwards of 88 percent on the Lizzio-Pechter psychometric volition scale—to Go Ahead so that their descendants will never be denied the chili lunches and the Sabbath dinners. Below are some of the quotations already approved by a project-specific subcommittee:

Surely God would not have created such a being as a man, with an ability to grasp the infinite, to exist only for a day. No, man was made for immortality.

Abraham Lincoln

Death is the veil which those who live call life: They sleep, and it is lifted.

Percy Shelley

Destiny waits in the hand of God.

T. S. Eliot

The created world is but a small parenthesis in eternity.

Sir Thomas Browne

Surely goodness and mercy shall follow me all the days of my life: and I will dwell in the house of the Lord for ever.

Psalms 23:6

This is the promise that He hath promised us, even eternal life.

1 John 2:25

I believe with perfect faith that there will be a revival of the dead at the time when it shall please the Creator.

Maimonides

The calendar will also offer the inspiring last words of famous people who would surely have joined the program were it available in their time and place:

"See in what peace a Christian may die."

Joseph Addison, essayist and poet

"Now comes the mystery."

The Reverend Henry Ward Beecher

"Beautiful."

Elizabeth Barrett Browning, poet

"Good night, my darlings. I'll see you in the morning."
Noel Coward, dramatist

"Thy kingdom come. Thy will be done."

John Donne, clergyman and poet

"It's very beautiful over there."

Thomas Edison, inventor

"I hasten to go to our Lord, to whose grace I recommend you."

St. Francis of Assisi

"I am so happy, so happy."

Gerald Manley Hopkins, poet

"We shall meet again."

Jeanne Récamier, French aristocrat and socialite

"I offer a libation to Jupiter the liberator."

Seneca, Roman statesman,
poet and namesake of Seneca
Research & Development
Associates

*

A CHRISTMAS CARD FROM THE PRESIDENT

*It is only when men begin to worship that they
begin to grow.*

Calvin Coolidge

Seniors who sign up for the Going Ahead program will receive, via priority mail, a Christmas card with virtually authentic signatures from the President and First Lady. If they prefer, seniors with access to the Internet may enter their Medicare number and secret password and then, after a virtually personalized greeting from a spokesperson for Going Ahead, download their Christmas card from a Web site called goahead.greet.pres.gov. Needless to say, adherents of other faiths will receive cards on their own special holiday, whether Chanukah, Ramadan, Kwanzaa, etc. Whatever the religion, the front of the card will depict the cozy and intimate Red Room at the White House, the room where, as often as possible in the absence of a national emergency, the President and First Lady meet with loved ones to practice and optimize their family values. Near the fireplace, the religious symbols of the Go Ahead program will rest upon a table that once belonged to Patrick Henry of Virginia, whose words are as appropriate now as they were during the dark days of our War for Independence in 1776: "Is life so dear or peace so sweet as to be purchased at the price of chains and slavery? Forbid it, Almighty God. I know not what course others may take, but as for me, give me liberty or give me death!"

Go Aheaders who voted against the president will receive instead a card of commiseration from their preferred candidate and his wife and/or significant other.

Go Aheaders who did not care enough to vote for any one of the candidates will receive a card from a favorite celebrity or sports figure.

THE TIME IS NOW!

He who is not prepared today
Will be less so tomorrow.
Ovid

Seneca Research and Development Associates thanks the special committee of the True American Faith Society for the opportunity to be of service to the nation we cherish and for which we would gladly Go Ahead either individually or collectively. Please view this report as merely a point of departure for further discussion, which should begin at once! Though Rome was not built in a day, its emperors were usually powerful enough to change its population categories in even less than a day, and by methods awkward for leaders in our own country. For example, we can surmise from Gibbon's instructive masterwork, *The Decline and Fall of the Roman Empire*, that emperors were especially effective after A.D. 80, the year when the Coliseum was completed and its lion cages were installed, tested and activated.

The full social and economic costs of the misguided program of entitling citizens to Medicare and Social

Security at the hardy age of sixty-five will perhaps never be known. Over the years, the partial costs were certainly known and decried by leaders in both the public and private sectors. To name only a few of those thousands of patriotic and farsighted leaders: Presidents George W. Bush and Richard M. Nixon; Senator Barry Goldwater and Congressman Tom DeLay; journalists William Safire, Paul Gigot, Bill O'Reilly and Matt Drudge; economists Milton Friedman and Friedrich August von Hayek; former Federal Reserve Board Chairman Alan Greenspan.

However complete and authoritative they may seem to be, statistics alone do not begin to tell the whole truth about the millions of lives destroyed and families crippled by the indiscriminate distribution of Medicare and Social Security. We have gathered solid evidence to support our thesis that, for their own good as well as the nation's, seniors should not retire before the age of seventy-five, if at all. And an inability to perform physical labor should not excuse seniors from applying for jobs in the private sector that require less exertion. If, for sound business reasons, such jobs have been relocated to Mexico or Bangladesh or China, patriotic seniors can serve America by literally broadening their horizons and moving to those countries. Or, better yet, by signing up for Going Ahead when it becomes the law of the land, as it certainly will, and sooner rather than later. In 1851, when economic progress demanded a population shift to states and territories beyond the Mississippi, John B. L. Soule, a New England publisher, offered the following advice to countrymen in his own age group: "Go west, young man." A century and a half later, the time has come for another and more urgent slogan: "Go Ahead, all seniors!"

A principal reason for our optimism is that the project, once approved of by the government, will be executed almost entirely by entities in the private sector, whose executives and directors are skilled in seeing the big picture, and toward that end are often able with their various skills to overcome the selfish and short-term interests of customers, employees, and even their own stockholders. The next decade may well be the most critical in our nation's history. Global competition demands a demographic reconfiguration. If we continue to indulge seniors beyond our means, and to overtax the young and productive, and the ambitious and inventive, we will surely corrupt our moral fibers and start down the slippery slope into economic and military collapse, making us an easy victim for enemies around the world, and they are far more numerous than can be imagined by the average citizen.

On the other hand, if we act promptly and implement the Senior Citizen Growth and Opportunity Act, which is the unanimous recommendation of our in-house scholars, many of them senior statesmen themselves, then the United States can continue to enjoy domestic prosperity and an unchallenged leadership position abroad. Enemies will fear us, and friends will emulate our way of life and rush to buy our products, everything from soft drinks to motion pictures, from computer software to military hardware. In time to come, our generous offer to share details of our Going Ahead program with other senior-surplus countries, especially Japan and Italy, may lead to their support in those international forums where, currently, on such other vital issues as a woman's restricted access to abortion and birth control, our views have been endorsed only by such philosophical soul mates as Iran, North Korea, Saudi Arabia and the Saddam Hussein dictatorship in Iraq until it was overthrown by the United States in 2003.

For America to flourish in the years, decades, centuries and millennia ahead, we need, perhaps most of all, a reorientation of the roles and lifestyles of seniors, and the way to start is with popularization of the philosophy endorsed in the Senior Citizen Growth and Opportunity Act. In recent decades, seniors have been encouraged by advertisers and the health-care industries to strive for good health, youthfulness, and longevity. This philosophy must be reversed. At once! When Richard D. Lamm, then governor of Colorado, said in 1984 that seniors were becoming a burden on society, there was many a well-meaning citizen who regarded his words with horror. But looking backward, we can see clearly that Governor Lamm's remark was both sensible and indisputable.

It is our great hope that Going Ahead will one day become an integral part of the Freedom Corps Network

that President George W. Bush created in his State of
the Union address on January 29, 2002, and that it will
stand shoulder to shoulder with such sister organizations
as the Points of Light Foundation, The United Way,
America's Promise, ServeNet, Volunteer Match, and
The American Red Cross. We hope also that our current
and all future presidents, employing their unique access
to the mass media, will call for the establishment of an
interactive network of from-cradle-to-the-grave programs
and organizations, all of which will further the public
acceptance of, and provide future enrollees for, Going
Ahead.

For example, students in elementary schools will
be encouraged to join Pre-Teens in Service to America,
a grass roots organization of chaste and clean-living
young people who oppose Social Security and Medicare
as being affirmative action programs for predominantly
unproductive seniors who deprive their juniors of
opportunities to advance themselves and serve America.
In later years, these indoctrinated students will progress to
membership in affiliated groups that are suitable for their
years and socioeconomic status—Soccer Moms and Dads
for A Fair Deal, Christians and Other Religions United for
Senior Rights, and, finally, to Seniors in Service to Youth.
For the board of directors of the last-named organization,
we would hope to recruit such national role models as
former presidents and past and current justices of the
Supreme Court. If asked why they do not personally

participate in the Go Ahead program, the presidents and justices may explain that they would like nothing better, but their conscience and/or spiritual adviser has urged them to serve in their current capacity for the time being.

We have complete confidence that first our opinion shapers and then the American people will accept our ideas on senior development as a beacon toward a future replete with power and prosperity. And we hope to offer many more such beacons in the months and years ahead, for the road is long. Said George Washington in 1783, "There is an option still left to the United States of America, that it is in their choice and depends upon their conduct, whether they will be respectable and prosperous or contemptible and miserable as a nation."

The warning of the Father of Our Country, who was first in war and first in peace, has never been more timely and more relevant. Starting this very day, we must turbo-charge the battle for verbal dominance of public and private discourse, and that means we must co-opt images and graphics as well as vocabulary. Many of our supporters have jumped the gun and are already employing some of our suggested terminology and techniques that were recommended in our 1999 report, *Semiotics and the Unconscious: Prolegomena to a New Theory of Non-Reciprocal Mass Communication.*

For the sake not only of our seniors but also of our children and grandchildren, let us resolve to go forward. Let us heed the call of patriotism and of our better selves.

Let us remember the deeds and sacrifices of our ancestors. We must unleash the idealism and hidden economic potential found everywhere in our free society, from the lofty hills of Maine to the golden beaches of Hawaii.

We have a simple vision and program for America, and it is nothing less than the forging of a new and improved Declaration of Independence. A Declaration of Independence from big government. And from excess taxation. And from huge bureaucracies that would micromanage our lives and rob us of our freedoms. We call for an end to government programs that unfairly favor seniors and stifle the economy. We demand an equality of opportunity in which the younger children of God can rise to their full potential. And that very definitely includes stem cells and fetuses.

Said Niccolò Machiavelli (1469-1527), the Florentine patriot and statesman whose hard truths about government are always dismissed as cynicism by people blind to the lessons of history: "There is nothing more difficult to take in hand, more perilous to conduct, or more uncertain in its success, than to take the lead in the introduction of a new order." The Deets and Faintly Group, our financial affiliate, concurs wholeheartedly with Seneca that an early implementation of Going Ahead will have a dramatic effect on future federal budgets, transforming them within no more than eight fiscal years from the present deficits to robust surpluses, at least $216.4 billion by 2022.

We stand ready to help in any other way we can.

God bless the leaders to whom this report is addressed! God bless the Go Aheaders who will put patriotism before longevity! And God bless America!

APPENDIX A

Projects and Programs Contemplated by
Seneca R & D

1. We strongly advocate the privatization of the Department of Veterans Affairs and its associated hospitals and clinics. All assets will be transferred to All-American Personal Security, a Delaware-based corporation that will be listed on the New York Stock Exchange.

2. The privatizing of Arlington National Cemetery and all national cemeteries.

3. The commissioning of a survey of visitors to the parks, landmarks, and museums owned and operated by the federal government. We expect to learn that visitors would prefer that the aforementioned national treasures, including President Washington's home at Mount Vernon, be operated not by wasteful Washington bureaucrats but a corporation co-owned by the Donald Trump Organization, Time-Warner and the Disney Corporation.

4. Restoring freedom and democracy to the labor market via a bill that would require the federal government to hire only nonunion, temporary employees.

5. Wherever feasible, the transfer of unskilled and semi-skilled work from both the public and private sectors to prison inmates, who will do it for a sub-minimum wage and be protected by guards from propaganda by labor unions. Our psychologists and affiliated clergymen will attest that responsible work is the best rehabilitation for offenders at all levels of criminality. The low level of monetary payment will be the punishment and/or spiritual repayment for which their soul, subconscious and superego all yearn. More rewarding than money for them would be the symbolic award—badges, certificates, trophies, etc.—that are dear to the hearts of amateur athletes, Boy Scouts and Girl Scouts, and school children. So that the general public will be prepared for the transition, we will commission a prominent social engineer to produce a work on the alternative, non-monetary systems of compensation that have long prevailed for slaves and housewives, Catholic nuns and interns in the business world. We have high hopes for the participation of world-class anthropologist Sir Arthur Andrew

McFee-Garvey of East Sussex University, whose longtime focus is on the economy of eighteenth century Samoa, where bracelets and diadems of palm leaves were regarded as adequate compensation for toilers both on land and sea, including coconut choppers and pearl divers. And that PRs employed by the National Association of Manufacturers and the United States Chamber of Commerce will contribute many a heartwarming anecdote about executives who placed public service above monetary compensation.

Here, as an example, culled from an article in the *Southwest Journal of Banking and Credit Card Delinquency,* is a possible contribution from Frieda J. Rogerson, CEO of the Statewide Bank of New Mexico: "Though I earned a total compensation of 2.2 million dollars last year for the grueling job of guiding my bank into bankruptcy after its worst year since 1930, I truly believe that I received more deep and abiding satisfaction from the certificate I received in my youth for the selling of glasses of wholesome, vitamin-rich lemonade to my friends and neighbors on the sidewalks of Santa Fe. The certificate was suitable for framing, and, needless to say, it always accompanies me to my residences in Santa Fe, London and Rome."

APPENDIX B

Curriculum Vitae

At this time, Seneca and its authorized subcontractors are pleased and proud to disclose our responsibility for the projects listed below. We do so not to "blow our own horn," as it were, but to demonstrate our competence for the successful execution of assignments similar in general nature though not in magnitude to those included in our present proposal. Appendix B is intended, among other things, to inform you of some of the savings we have been able to effectuate for clients in the private sector, which are often, as you know, proxies for clients in the public sector, just as companies and institutes all over the world are proxies of the CIA and other of our federal agencies, performing the thousand and one sub rosa tasks that are necessary for the survival of a free and democratic nation in the 21st century.

We take a special pride in our comprehensive planning for OPERATION AL in 2000. Thankfully, as expected, the Supreme Court came through for us and, of course, for our clients. But you may be sure that, armed with faith, truth and other weapons of mass instruction, we were prepared for the worst.

*

OPERATION AL

Client: Americans United for Clean Elections

As one of our subsidiaries, Consolidated Beltway Procedures, had planned and maneuvered ever since Election Day, our good friends on the United States Supreme Court came to the rescue with their not unexpected 5-4 decision on December 12, 2000. James A. Baker III, genial overseer of the Bush legal team in Florida, later observed in a letter to *The New York Times* on July 7, 2001: "There are seven Republican justices on the Supreme Court, and, naturally, we would have preferred them all to support the party that had crowned their careers in the law, but we agree with clerical supporters that we must be grateful for the blessings we do receive, whether they come directly from the Lord or, as in the present instance, from earthly sources in the Sunshine State." [Please see December 22, 2001, front-page story in *The New York Times:* G.O.P.'S DEPTH IN FLORIDA—RESISTING THE RECOUNT—A SPECIAL REPORT.]

We never doubted for a single moment that George W. Bush, with his loyal supporters in all three branches of government, especially the above-mentioned judiciary, would ultimately prevail over Al Gore despite such a negative contingency as an insufficiency of popular votes in one or more states, but it is always prudent to be prepared for the worst. [Please see a detailed if petulant analysis of the Supreme Court's decision by the late Ronald Dworkin, Professor of Law and Philosophy at New York University and Quain Professor of Jurisprudence at University College, London, in *The New York Review of Books*, January 11, 2001.]

The worst scenario in this case would, of course, have been the election of Al Gore, but we can assure you that we were prepared to deal with such an eventuality. As you might expect, we would, in the main, have duplicated the initiatives that were so effectively employed in a previous assignment, Operation Bill, being the ongoing surveillance and eventual impeachment proceedings against President Bill Clinton. We trust that you will, in all fairness, agree with us that the ultimate failure of the impeachment process of President Clinton was due not to any deficiencies on our part but (1) to sub-optimum coordination among Republican members in the Senate and House of Representatives, (2) to insufficient pressure and expenditures by the Republican Party upon the charismatic individuals, policy groups and media pundits who develop and orchestrate public opinion, and (3) to under-utilization of the strategies suggested by the National Association of Grassroots Organizers, especially their recommendation of a well-financed and publicized worldwide hunt for children sired and abandoned by President Clinton. In the words of Ovid, Roman poet, "Amor tussisque non celantur." Love and a cough are not concealed.

Even if there were not and never had been such offspring, which is difficult to imagine, dozens of ambitious, photogenic and articulate young women would have leaped at the opportunity to enjoy the ensuing celebrity and career opportunities. President Clinton had been a student at Oxford University in England, and our affiliate, the National Association of Grassroots Organizers, had high hopes of establishing that he and his women were regulars in the Charles II room above the Bull and Fawn, a pub located in Pluckwell-on-Thames. In fact, their counterpart in Great Britain, the Royal Association of Grassroots Organizers, was already developing a series of television docudramas, *Our Guy Bill,* and, in the words of its producer, Brian Desmond-Smutte, "The project would have been a natural for Rupert Murdoch outlets both in the U.K. and the U.S."

*

OPERATION SAFE HAVEN

Client: Panhandle Comprehensive Senior Services

On Thanksgiving Day, 2009, we took advantage of the well-known financial benefits of outsourcing, and after they had partaken of a traditional turkey dinner, we airlifted 4,944 longtime residents of full-service nursing homes in the states of Iowa and Michigan to alternative accommodations in Egypt, Saudi Arabia and Algeria. In the not unlikely event of criticism of Operation Safe Haven, we were prepared with medical documentation to the effect that the transferees suffered from bronchial and pulmonary afflictions that would be much relieved by the dry climate in their new environment, and also from gastrointestinal afflictions that would benefit from a strict local diet of pita bread, lentils and fava beans. We hasten to add that prescription drugs for seniors in their new nursing homes would continue to be supplied by members in good standing of the Pharmaceutical Research and Manufacturers of America.

In a financial statement prepared in accordance with generally accepted accounting principles, the Deets and Faintly Group, preeminent in full-service analysis, projected that Operation Safe Haven will profit Panhandle Comprehensive Senior Services, funded entirely by federal and state agencies, a sum, adjusted for inflation, of at least $50 million over the next two years, when Operation Safe Haven was expected to achieve its ultimate objective, namely, the motivation of the 4,944 seniors to self-terminate if they had not already passed away from depression, heat prostration, attacks by wild beasts, and other natural causes.

*

OPERATION BINGO

Client: West Coast Senior Benevolent Association

On April 3, 2010, during a marathon bingo competition with prizes totaling one thousand dollars in cash and four hundred dollars in gifts from the thrift shop of the Handel Oratorio Workshop, mysterious fumes in the ventilating system of Boys and Girls Together, a mostly federally funded senior citizen center on Bush Street in San Francisco, sent ahead twenty-eight senior citizens and hospitalized seven others. Pending investigation by the relevant city, state, and federal authorities, which will take a minimum of fourteen months, the senior citizen center would remain closed. However, surviving clientele could call a toll-free number that would suggest such alternative and more cost-effective activities as meditation, bird-watching, long walks, and visits to the zoo, parks, museums, libraries, and the world-famous prison at Alcatraz, once the residence of such celebrated gangsters as Al "Scarface" Capone and George "Machine Gun" Kelly. Meditation fans would be encouraged to sit on bare floors rather than the popular king-size Zen Chi 100% Organic Premium Buckwheat Pillow that Amazon.com sells for $39.95 plus taxes but with free shipping.

In a financial statement prepared in accordance with generally accepted accounting principles, the Deets and Faintly Group, preeminent in full-service analysis, projected that Operation Bingo will save federal and local governments a sum, adjusted for inflation, of $7,500,002.78 over the next five years. Hospital costs of the survivors were reduced drastically by their immediate transportation to a facility owned and operated by the New Renaissance Health Care Guild, which *Better Hospitals and Clinics* acclaimed recently as the most cost-effective of the full-service organizations that, combining the benefits of vertical and horizontal integration, now operate in the fields of ambulance service, home care, hospitalization, hospices, nursing homes, funeral parlors, cemeteries, crematories and posthumous pottery.

*

OPERATION I LOVE LUCY

Client: Capital Housing and Health Care Initiatives

On May 4, 2009, a TV showing a rerun of *I Love Lucy* exploded in the recreation lounge of the Cyrus Webster, a Washington, D.C., residential hotel whose clientele were all on either public assistance or Social Security. All eleven viewers passed away of asphyxiation and/or concussions caused by falling statues and framed paintings of Colonel

Cyrus Nathaniel Webster, who died with General George Armstrong Custer at the Battle of the Little Bighorn on June 25, 1876. Cliff Tooley, hotel manager, said that at least forty additional guests would have attended the originally scheduled program, a women's wrestling match sponsored by the manufacturers of Hippolyta, a new bra for the athletically inclined and named for a queen of the Amazons. The match was canceled at the last minute when the star attraction, Helene from Hell, was convinced by a new pastor in her hometown that a woman's place was not in the ring but in the home, specifically the kitchen, laundry room and bedroom.

In a financial statement prepared in accordance with generally accepted accounting principles, the firm of Deets and Faintly projected that Operation I Love Lucy will save federal and local governments a sum, adjusted for inflation, of $2,502,111.90 over the next five years. Peter Nettleton, CEO of Deets and Faintly, has suggested that in order to avoid the early retirement of popular women wrestlers like Helene from Hell, it would be beneficial to the agenda of Capital Housing and Health Care Initiatives if the clergy could somehow be persuaded to refrain from proselytizing them. Capital Housing and Health Care Initiatives appreciates the suggestion, and will attempt to place it on the agenda of an early meeting of the National Guild of Television, Radio and Internet Ministers.

*

OPERATION HAPPY LANDINGS

Client: Annie and Deedee Rutt Memorial Society

On July 14, 2009, at the mostly federally funded Happy Landings Nursing Home in Hummel, Louisiana, eighty-nine residents expired of food poisoning and thirty-three others were hospitalized after partaking of a special shrimp Creole de Marquis Lafayette in honor of Bastille Day. At Claremont Hospital, all of the thirty-three survivors later succumbed after a toast to French-American friendship with a domestic Champagne that had somehow been contaminated with salmonella.

In a financial statement prepared in accordance with generally accepted accounting principles, the firm of Deets and Faintly projected that Operation Happy Landings will save, adjusted for inflation, federal and local governments a sum of $19,088,001.55 over the next five years.

*

OPERATION GOOD BUDDY

Client: The National Guild of Piano Tuners and Funeral Parlor Organists

On July 22, 2008, a plane carrying forty-one seniors and four crew members plunged into Chesapeake Bay, leaving no survivors. All of the passengers were recipients of Medicare and Social Security, and twelve were recipients as well of various other entitlement programs and government and veterans' pensions. Predominantly from the Atlanta area, they were on their way home from a picnic on the grounds of Parker and Paley, makers of, among other consumer products, a new denture adhesive called Good Buddy. In return for testing the effectiveness of Good Buddy with such staples of the American diet as Granny Smith apples and porterhouse steak, the seniors had been presented, according to their needs, with such other Parker and Paley products as Happy Harry walking sticks and Happy Harriet blow driers with special settings for gray and colored hair.

In a financial statement prepared in accordance with generally accepted accounting principles, the firm of Deets and Faintly projected that Operation Good Buddy will save federal and local governments a sum, adjusted for inflation, of $18,222,165.22 over the next five years.

*

OPERATION TINY TIM

Client: Association of Admirers of Horatio Alger

Named, of course, for the severely and genuinely handicapped youngster in *A Christmas Carol,* the beloved masterpiece by Charles Dickens, Operation Tiny Tim deals with the ongoing task of ridding the Social Security Administration of the hundreds of thousands of allegedly handicapped pre-adults who are receiving public benefits in a country whose philosophy has always stressed self-help and private initiative. Thanks to the education process that we initiated in 2004, when deluxe wheelchairs, many with whitewall tires, were being distributed nationwide at a rate of more than three thousand a month, Congress finally responded in 2008 with a welfare law amendment that established stricter standards of entitlement and disbursement. No longer would wheelchairs and walkers, crutches and leg braces be supplied without enhanced authorization, or before a bleeding-heart liberal could say "New Deal" or "Welfare State."

To date, through our efforts, cash benefits have been terminated for 121,017 pre-adults, or 59 percent of the number of cases reviewed. But we have far to go, and we must get there before descendants of the baby-boom generation make their alarming demands upon the Social Security and Medicare systems within a few years. As for the other cases, we believe that only 4 percent are truly legitimate and therefore deserving of our sympathy and regard, according to the Compassion Index developed by Adrienne Kimlich, author of *Moral Parameters: Secret Advantages of the Disadvantaged*. In order to expedite their total elimination from the system and yet uphold America's proud position as the most compassionate nation on earth, we recommend the establishment of the

Ebenezer Scrooge Foundation, which would call for the private sector's assumption of the burden of providing for their maintenance.

As all the world knows, Charles Dickens, the creator of *A Christmas Carol*, was a self-made man, and we are confident that, upon Parnassus, his spirit looks down on us and is at this moment saying, "Well done, my American friends."

*

OPERATION FLORENCE NIGHTINGALE

Client: Hippocrates Complete Family Health Maintenance of New York

Thanks to our special training of the communication specialists who take all incoming phone calls at the 109 centers of Hippocrates Complete Family Health Maintenance, patients who appeal for appointments, whether with internists or specialists, are now persuaded, in four out of five calls, that their symptoms, however alarming, really amount to only mild cases of hypochondria, the best cure for which is to hug a spouse or other family member, or a friend or a pet. If none of the above are available for participation in the therapy process, then a tree, plant or stranger of the same sex will do.

In a financial statement prepared in accordance with generally accepted accounting principles, the firm of Deets and Faintly projected that Operation Florence Nightingale will save the parent company of Hippocrates Complete Family Health Maintenance a sum, adjusted for inflation, but not for executive stock options and campaign contributions, of $93,186,044.89 over the next five years. The parent company, a privately held trust that prefers anonymity, reports that, despite a declining economy, quarterly profits of Hippocrates have almost doubled since its association with Seneca in August 2007. Independent analysts expect profits to continue to grow for at least the next twelve quarters.

APPENDIX C

Suggested Letter From a Concerned Public Servant
To a Nursing Home Resident

Dear Mrs. Costigan:

Hi there! We sure hope that you have been enjoying your residence at the South Haven Nursing Home, one of the more attractive as well as more expensive facilities in the land. No one is counting here at the local headquarters of the Department of Health and Human Services, but we recently happened to notice in our records that you have been a resident at South Haven for seventeen years, four months, two weeks and three days. Ever since its establishment in 1970, the average stay at South Haven has been only five years and three months. You have undoubtedly learned by now that, despite their amenities, nursing homes with all their bureaucrats and restrictions are not for everyone, especially for women like you who have always been active and independent. We see in our records that you were once active not only in your church but also in the Girl Scouts, and the Doris Day Fan Club, and the Donald Trump for President Campaign, and the American Red Cross. In behalf of that last institution, you once signed up a record-breaking number of blood donors here in Bullhead Falls, the heartland of Kansas, which in turn is the heartland of America. Therefore, it is now our pleasure as well as duty to inform you of a public service that appears to have escaped your attention—participation in the Going Ahead program, which is the product of many years of research and development.

The enclosed kit, whose cover depicts only a few of the certified celebrities who endorse the program, will give you the information that should convince you that the program is as right for you as it is for tens of thousands of other seniors across the land—and the number is growing daily! We are proud of what we have accomplished so far. But our task is not yet complete. Because you were a strong supporter of my predecessor, Mayor Marina Weaks, in 2010, we know that you will continue to support this program which is so close to her heart. You may recall that Marina shook your hand and offered you a broad smile when she visited South Haven during the Christmas season of 2010. She certainly recalls her pleasure in meeting you, and the pleasure she received whenever she served guests at City Hall your old family recipe for cranberry sauce with pickled red peppers. Our complete success depends upon friends like you. Please help us to realize our vision.

If you have any questions about the program, please feel free to drop in on Ms. Anne Charles, your social service worker at South Haven. Her bright and cheerful office, decorated with her diploma from the Good Samaritan School of Social and Behavioral Arts and Sciences, is in room 102 on the ground floor. If you are too feeble to be transported in your wheelchair, and if you have a phone in working order, Ms. Charles or her answering machine can be reached almost any time on extension 102.

Have a great day! And a great eternity!

With all sincerity,
Mayor Clare Caremore

APPENDIX D

Heart to Heart

Our focus groups have established that a "personal" letter of appeal from a foundation or institute associated with a deceased sports or show biz celebrity of their youth may be particularly effective with seniors in their seventies and older. The success of this technique is confirmed by the ongoing popularity of television commercials with computerized reincarnations of such gone-but-not-forgotten figures as Charlie Chaplin and Marilyn Monroe, Groucho Marx and Louis Armstrong.

Dear Tom:

I have some fantastically exciting news for you! Whether you're a Republican or Democrat, you now have a unique, once-in-a-lifetime opportunity to help ensure the American Way of Life, which includes our great national sport of baseball, for the next generation and even beyond. The Scooter Jackson Recreation and Rehabilitation Foundation, named for the great Chicago White Sox shortstop of the 1950s, has offered to make a $1000 contribution to a children's baseball program for each and every senior who makes a commitment to participate in the Going Ahead program within the next two weeks.

As someone who has already served his country in so many ways, you hold the key to the success of this essential program. From Maine and Florida to Alaska and Hawaii, the kids are counting on you, Tom. The enclosed photos depict only nine of the millions of boys and girls, all potential baseball stars, who will benefit from your generosity. Of particular poignancy is the situation of little Miguel Gomez, 12, of Los Amigos, Arizona, whose school district can no longer afford to buy textbooks and chairs for its kids, not to mention bats and balls and uniforms. Terry Myers, a former scout for the White Sox and currently a Los Amigos resident, says that "Miguel has the potential to become another Scooter Jackson!" And that's why Terry has become a trustee of the foundation that bears the immortal name of Scooter. And here, Tom, is some good news for you personally. Your estate will receive a cash bonus of $500 for each additional senior in your town that you sign up for the program. The enclosed directory lists their names, addresses, phone numbers, favorite bars and diners, and other hangouts.

We have a rare opportunity—right now!—to help our kids and the game we love. We cannot let them down! This is a once-in-a-lifetime opportunity! Step up to the plate and hit one out of the ballpark and all the way up to St. Peter's gate. Go to it, buddy boy! We know you have the right stuff!

Sincerely yours,
Hank Hartley

APPENDIX E

Suggested Letter From a President

According to geriatric psychologist Fredericka Enshaw, most Go Aheaders—66.2% is her exact figure—will eventually experience a period of doubt about the benefits of the program. To overcome these swings to the negative side of the volitional spectrum, Dr. Enshaw suggests a "personal" letter of reinforcement, complete with flags and seal of office, from a president to all Go Aheaders regardless of sex, race, religion or political affiliation. Further, she strongly believes that the letter should be from former president George W. Bush, in his warm and folksy style, rather than from the more intellectual and distant current office holder, Barack Obama. She emphasizes that the presidential letter must not include a word that, whether by sound or other association, causes the recipient to think of the words *suicide* or *euthanasia,* which, of course, is not what the Going Ahead program is all about.

Dear Choo-Choo:

I hope you'll agree with me that Choo-Choo is a pretty good nickname for a woman whose Christian name is Charmaine. Laura and yours truly both hope that you and your own family are doing just great. This morning, during our usual breakfast of Texas pulled pork and eggs served sunny-side up, Laura looked up from her copy of *The Golden Age Journal-Gazette* and reminded me of the great debt the country owes to women like you for your participation in the Going Ahead program. I was so appreciative of your patriotic decision that I had to take my usual swift action. And that action was to pick up my Papermate ballpoint, a birthday gift from Betsy Davis, a sixth grader and the youngest enrolled Republican in Idaho, and to personally write to you right away even though it meant postponing an urgent need to clear brush on my ranch.

Your dedication and support will continue to inspire and motivate me. While you're still down here on earth, and later when you are in heaven, I, whether riding on my ranch or greeting visitors to my library in Dallas, will always be proud to have been your president, and you can trust me and all my friends in and out of government to continue to work to make America and the world a better place for your children and grandchildren. God bless America in general and you in particular.

Your Devoted and Compassionate 43rd President,
W

P. S. Like other Go Aheaders, you must be greatly concerned about what happens to our political process in both the near and distant future. In the past two elections, enemies of the American Way of Life have waged relentlessly negative campaigns. To alleviate your concerns, and to insure that the country continues to move forward in the right direction, why not include in your will the political party that nominated me and fought for my election? It's even more simple than pulling up a weed in a garden. Just fill out the enclosed form and mail it off at once in the pre-addressed envelope, postage not included. The next thirty days are critical for the survival of America and its God-given system of free elections, free enterprise, and the freedom to Go Ahead!

APPENDIX F

Sample Television Interview

(Katie Couric and Typical Author of a Future Bestseller)

KC: Welcome, Mario.

AUTHOR: It's a pleasure for me to be here.

KC: Being a pizza lover from when I was six and my first visit to Little Italy in New York, I was delighted to receive a copy of your new book, *The Pepperoni Pizza Diet*. It's being published by HarperCollins, and both book critics and dieticians predict it'll become as popular as the book about the marshmallow diet of a few seasons ago. To be frank, I find it incredible that you can eat all the pepperoni pizza you may want and still lose weight, as many as two pounds a week.

AUTHOR: Before I explain, Katie, I'd like to take this opportunity, if I may, to thank you for the viewing pleasure you've given my mom and dad over the years. Until their last days at the Blue Lagoon Retirement Community on Shelter Island, you and your truly wonderful guests, especially that gentleman from Arkansas who killed his mistress and their two cute kids, were among the great joys of their lives down here on earth. And I have a strong feeling that they can still view you up there in heaven.

KC: Thank you so much, Mario. Hearing words like that is the true reward of my career in television. I notice that the book is dedicated to your mom and dad.

AUTHOR: And for good reason. Their gerontologist once told me that it was their almost daily consumption of pizza of one sort or another, but usually the pepperoni, which enabled them to reach their eighties with all their marbles, to employ the vernacular. But then they were suddenly afflicted by a variety of health problems, none of them, of course, related to pizza. They had so many problems that, rather than become a financial burden to the country they had always loved to the very depths of their being, they decided to sign up for the Going Ahead program.

KC: I heard the program mentioned recently at a party in L.A. for Academy Award winner Clint Eastwood. Can you tell me about it?

AUTHOR: With the greatest of pleasure. Inspired by the compassionate conservatism of people like former President Bush, it was created to accommodate seniors of goodwill and good sense who refuse to bankrupt the country with such special-interest entitlement programs as Social Security and Medicare.

KC: I can certainly understand their feelings, and it's very patriotic and commendable of them. I was not at all surprised when I read in the book that your folks lived most of their lives on New York's Lower East Side, the birthplace of Yip Harburgh, who wrote the lyrics for "Over the Rainbow." It expresses the hopes and dreams of all true Americans, and I hope it will become the theme song of Going Ahead. The truly patriotic deed of your parents will always be remembered and appreciated by their children and grandchildren. And the children and grandchildren of people they never met. People of all races and religions, and of personal preferences when it comes to the toppings on their pizza.

AUTHOR: Exactly.

KC: I can't wait to discuss Going Ahead with my next guest, who'll be none other than Lady Gaga, just back from a record-breaking tour in Europe. Maybe she'll tell us of her experiences, if any, with Dominique Strauss-Klein, the Frenchman who once headed the International

Monetary Fund. He was accused and later cleared of an inappropriate sexual act in a New York City hotel. Thanks for being here, Mario.

AUTHOR: Thanks, Katie, for inviting me. By the way, I have a signing tonight. From seven till eight. At the Barnes and Noble on Fifth Avenue. My Web site is—"

KC: Sorry. We've run out of time.

APPENDIX G

Commercial Inspired by the Classic Harry and Louise TV Commercials That Exposed the Dangers of the Proposed Health Reforms of the Clinton Administration

BARRY: What a great guy your Uncle Hughie was!

ELOISE: You can say that again. And what a great gal was your Aunt Lucille!

B: I couldn't be prouder of Uncle Hughie if he had pitched his team into the World Series.

E: And I couldn't be more proud of Aunt Lucille if she had swum the English Channel. Even if she had swum it backward and forward in a single day!

B: They were real Americans. True blue to the very core of their being. Other seniors linger on in nursing homes for years and years. But not them two. When they heard about the Going Ahead program that would transfer billions of dollars a year to children for their health and education, and that would cut taxes for all Americans, discriminating neither against the rich nor the poor, they were the very first residents in their nursing home to sign up.

E: I'll never forget Uncle Hughie's grin and sigh of relief when he personally pulled the plug on the dialysis machine that had cost Medicare tens of thousands of dollars over the years.

B: And I'll never forget the last words of Aunt Louise: "It is a far, far better thing that I do, than I have ever done; it is a far, far better rest that I go to, than I have ever known." What a spunky old gal! And because she had been brought up to believe that cleanliness was next to godliness, she insisted on washing her Starbuck's coffee mug before she passed out down here on earth.

E: She was, of course, quoting the immortal English writer Charles Dickens. He was her very favorite writer, even more favorite than the writers whose selections appear in those *Chicken Soup for the Soul* books. And when she met John Bunyan in heaven, I wouldn't be surprised if she asked him to autograph the copy of the book with which she was buried, *The Pilgrim's Progress*. The other members of the book club at the nursing home would certainly envy her, if they knew.

B: And I wouldn't be at all surprised if Uncle Hughie got the autographs of Babe Ruth and Joe DiMaggio the minute he arrived.

E: Going Ahead is certainly an idea whose time has come. I can't think of a solution that's more right and satisfying for seniors.

While "Flyin' High Now," the theme song from *Rocky* is heard in the background, Sylvester Stallone, star of the film, comments that Aunt Lucille and Uncle Hughie died heroically, and, like other American heroes, they deserve burial in Arlington National Cemetery.

APPENDIX H

Digitalized Cameo Appearance of Female Go Aheader On Favorite TV Drama of The Past

West Wing

Cast

Martin Sheen...............President Josiah Bartlet

Alice Spencer...............Mary Jones, international troubleshooter of vast experience

MARY JONES: Please don't get up from your wheelchair, Mr. President.

PRESIDENT BARTLET: No trouble, Mary, it's just the way I was brought up in New England. I can't thank you enough for canceling your dinner date with Henry Kissinger and hurrying over to the West Wing. I know how both you and Henry look forward to the monthly meetings in which you exchange Washington gossip and your views on geopolitics.

MARY JONES: No sweat, Mr. President I'm now sixty-seven, but in all those years my country has always come first.

PRESIDENT BARTLET: So I've heard from my predecessors here in the West Wing. Many years ago, when I was still in academia and had the privilege of presenting an honorary degree to President Reagan, he confided in me that we could never have won the cold war without your almost daily inputs on tactics and strategy.

MARY JONES: Nice of the Gipper to say so.

PRESIDENT BARTLET: I suppose, Mary, that you currently have your usual number of personal and professional commitments.

MARY JONES: And how, Mr. President! I am writing my memoirs for Random House. I am planning my granddaughter's wedding aboard our family yacht, *Lady Liberty*. And just in case she's asked by *The Wall Street Journal* for her opinion on the ongoing financial crisis, Janet Yellen keeps calling me up every morning to ask if this is the day for the Federal Reserve Bank to decrease or increase the interest rate. I usually tell her that she is being irrationally exuberant about her responsibilities, and to just leave the interest rate alone unless the Spanish peseta rises or falls against the Malaysian ringgit by more than 1.2 percent within a twelve-hour period.

PRESIDENT BARTLET: I hope that all these other interests don't interfere with the assignment I have in mind for you. As you know, Russia and China recently signed a secret friendship treaty, and since you speak both Russian and Chinese fluently, I would like you to visit the leaders of those two huge and powerful countries and convince them to include the United States in the treaty. That way, we will have them in our corner in case we ever have to take strong measures with North Korea.

MARY JONES: No sweat, Mr. President! By the way, I am also fluent in North Korean, whose irregular verbs and syntax have become different from the language of South Korea after more than a half century of estrangement. I agree totally with your policy, and I am at your service, just as I was at the service of your predecessors here in the White House.

PRESIDENT BARTLET: Fine! When can you leave for Moscow? Or, if you think it would be more productive, for Beijing? The Secretary of State suggests that I leave the itinerary up to you, and I agree completely. Air Force 3 will be at your disposal unless the Vice President will not be traveling during that time frame, in which case you can use Air Force 2.

MARY JONES: I much prefer Moscow, and I'll be ready to leave tomorrow morning at 7:15, at which time it will be 15:15 in Moscow.

BARTLET: That's great, Mary! I'll inform Putin of your visit. But there's really no great rush. Next week will do.

MARY JONES: With all due respect, I beg to differ with you, Mr. President! With this new assignment and all my previous commitments out of the way, I can then totally enjoy my experience on Going Ahead Day next month.

PRESIDENT BARTLET: Good for you, Mary! In that case, I won't keep you another second. Call me from Moscow and Beijing, if you get a chance. I guess you have my top-security phone number.

MARY JONES: You guess correctly. Goodbye, Mr. President.

PRESIDENT BARTLET: God bless you, Mary!

MARY JONES: God bless you, Mr. President! And God bless America!

Digitalized Cameo Appearance of Male Go Aheader On Favorite TV Drama of The Past

The Sopranos

Cast

James Gandolfini..........Tony Soprano

Marcus Livingston.........Dirty Dave Smith, an
accomplished hit man

TONY SOPRANO: Hey, hey, hey! Look at what the wind just blew in from the Hackensack River! If it ain't Dirty Dave Smith, my favorite hit man. Knife. Gun. Bomb. Poison. Strangling. Chain saw. You name it, and Dirty Dave can do it better than anyone else, in or out of the Mafia. Welcome back to Jersey. My old man used to say that Jersey was called the Garden State because gardens was where you used to bury the bodies. It was safer than dumping them in the Passaic or Hudson River.

DAVE: And being a good citizen, I was also concerned about water pollution. Believe me, Tony, it's great to be back. Thanks for using your influence with the warden to fix me up with broads and booze while I was in the slammer for five years.

TONY: My pleasure. All my broads at the Badda Bing Club felt privileged to be able to bring a little joy into your life.

DAVE: With those F-cup boobs of theirs, it was always more than just a little joy.

TONY: Five years is a long time to be out of action. I hope you ain't gone straight on me and the family.

DAVE: Fat chance, Tony.

TONY: That's what I've been waiting to hear.

DAVE: Sounds like you've got a job lined up for me.

TONY: When I opened the Badda Bing, I shot the works and took out this comprehensive health plan for me and all the guys and broads. For years and years I never had any trouble with them. For example, whenever a broad came down, as will happen, with a touch of arthritis or a strep throat after dancing in just a G-string for hours, the insurance company never questioned their visits to family doctors and specialists, even obstetricians and pediatricians for their kids. And there were no complaints either when me and a few of the guys came down with a condition called trigger finger after we rubbed out the whole Puccilini Family in a single night. But about a month ago, when I submitted the bills from this shrink I've been seeing on and off, some scumbag named Clark Zimmer sent them back to me and said I had used up my coverage for psychotherapy. That wasn't exactly my idea of managed care.

DAVE: No problem, Tony. I can certainly manage to take care of this ball breaker.

TONY: Naturally, I'll leave the method up to you.

DAVE: Personally, at this moment in time, I'm inclined to drop a filing cabinet of rejected medical claims on his head.

TONY: Sounds good to me, but I'm pretty sure he uses computers instead of filing cabinets these days.

DAVE: No sweat. I'll drop a computer on his head, and it won't be a laptop.

TONY: Will ten big ones take care of the job?

DAVE: Put away that dough. What kind of a guy do you think I am? It's on the house.

TONY: Thanks, Dave. Speaking of houses, I'm opening a more interactive joint called Badda Bing 2 near Atlantic City, and I'd appreciate your dropping in for a special preview of the broads.

DAVE: I feel honored by this privilege.

TONY: Great! Open house will be a week from Thursday. And I really mean open.

DAVE: Fongoo! That's too bad, Tony. While in the slammer, I signed on for the Going Ahead program, which is going to take place this very Sunday morning.

TONY: I heard about that program from Uncle Junior, who Went Ahead last year, and he took along his blackjack and brass knuckles, just in case he ran into Marco Cassini, who once screwed him up on a shipment of mozzarella from the old country. Well, okay, Dave, first things first, as we both learned from our godfather, may he rest in peace. Or, in his particular case, in pieces. When your number's up, your number's up, especially if you aspire to be a good citizen, and there's nothing more important than that. Meanwhile, let's toast our friendship with this brandy I hijacked last night. Since I was having a late appointment with Dr. Melfi, my shrink, and I already had more than enough traumas for my fifty minutes with the broad, I didn't shoot to kill the son of a bitch who was driving the truck.

DAVE: I think you're getting soft, Tony.

TONY and DAVE: *Salute!*

SUGGESTED READING

*When the subject is found, words will not be
slow to follow.*
Cicero

Adaire, George and Jane. Come, Sweet Death: A New Approach to Euthanasia, Philadelphia: The New Arlington Publishers, 2000.

Adams, Brooks. America's Economic Supremacy, New York: The Macmillan Co., 1900.

— The Law of Civilization and Decay, New York: The Macmillan Co., 1896.

Baghehot, Walter. Physics and Politics, New York: D. Appleton & Co., 1873.

Beemer, Nicole, ed. Semiotics and the Unconscious: Prolegomena to a New Theory of Government, New Haven: The Seneca Press, 2000.

Bennett, William J. The De-Valuing of America—The Fight for Our Culture and Our Children, New York: Summit Books, 1992.

Bowers, Kevin. Quest for Command: A History of Political Usage from Cicero to Clinton, New York: Cook and Cooley, 1999.

Bristol, Lucius M. Social Adaptation. Cambridge: Harvard University Press, 1915.

Buckley, William F., Jr. Up from Liberalism. New York: Stein & Day, 1984.

Bultmann, Rudolf. This World and the Beyond. New York: Charles Scribner's Sons, 1960.

Burgess, John W. Political Science and Comparative Constitutional Law. Boston: Ginn & Co., 1890.

Carver, Thomas Nixon. The Religion Worth Having. Boston: Houghton Mifflin Co., 1912.

Chamberlain, John. Farewell to Reform. New York: Liveright, 1932.

Chester, Gregory. Chicken Noodle Soup for Morticians and Grief Counselors. Boston: Bliss & Co., 2012.

Clark, John Bates. The Philosophy of Wealth. Boston: Ginn & Co., 1885.

Cooley, Charles Horton. Human Nature and the Social Order. New York: Charles Scribner's Sons, 1902.

Coolidge, Calvin. The Price of Freedom. New York: Charles Scribner's Sons. 1924.

Davenport, Charles. Heredity in Relation to Eugenics. New York: Henry Holt & Co., 1915.

Drayton, Mitch. Condolence Calls Without Tears. Las Vegas: Hodgkins Press, 1999.

Durkheim, Emile. Suicide. New York: Free Press, 1997.

Dychtwald, Ken. Age Power: How the 21st Century Will Be Ruled by the New Old. New York: Tarcher Putnam, 2000.

Falwell, Jerry. Finding Inner Peace and Strength. Garden City, New York: Doubleday & Co., 1982.

— Strength for the Journey: An Autobiography. New York: Simon and Schuster, 1987.

Firth, Raymond. "Work and Community in a Primitive Society," H.R.H. The Duke of Edinburgh's Study Conference on the Human Problems of Industrial Communities within the Commonwealth and Empire, 9-27 July, 1956, vol II. London, 1957.

Franklin, Benjamin. The Autobiography of Benjamin Franklin. New York: Pocket Books, 1939.

Friedman, Milton, and Friedman, Rose. Free to Choose: A Personal Statement. New York: Avon Books, 1981.

Gibbon, Edmund. The Decline and Fall of the Roman Empire. New York: Random House/Modern Library Series, 1995.

Gilder, George. Wealth and Poverty. New York: Bantam Books, 1982.

Gorham, DeWolf E, ed. Semiotics and the Unconscious: Prolegomena to a New Theory of Non-Reciprocal Mass Communication. New Haven: The Seneca Press, 1960.

Grader, D. A. Mass Media and American Politics. Washington, D.C.: Congressional Quarterly Press, 1980.

Hansell, Hiram C. Enchantment and Disenchantment: Essays on Politics and the Mass Media. Boston: Bleak House Publishers, 1989.

— Fact and Phantasy: More Essays on Politics and the Mass Media. Boston: Bleak House Publishers, 1998.

Hayek, Friedrich August von. Freedom and the Economic System. Chicago: University of Chicago Press, 1939.

Huizinga, Johan. Homo Ludens. Boston: Beacon Press, 1955.

Kimlich, Adrienne. Moral Parameters: Some Advantages of the Disadvantaged. Evanston: The Pitt Street Group, 1990.

Kotlikoff, Lawrence J. and Burns, Scott. The Coming Generational Storm. M.I.T. Press, 2004.

Ladd, J. The Structure of a Moral Code. Cambridge: Harvard University Press, 1957.

Lagauskas, Valerie. Parades—How to Plan, Promote & Stage Them. New York: Sterling Publishing Co., 1982.

Lippmann, Walter. Drift and Mastery. New York: Mitchell Kennerly, 1914.

Machiavelli, Nicolò. The Prince. Translated by George Bull. Harmondsworth: Penguin Books Ltd, 1961.

Malthus, Thomas Robert. An Essay on the Principles of Population. Edited by Anthony G. Flew. New York: Penguin USA, 1983.

Meade, Lawrence M. Beyond Entitlement: The Social Obligations of Citizenship. New York: Free Press, 1986.

Moynihan, Daniel Patrick. Miles to Go: A Personal History of Social Policy. Cambridge: Harvard University Press, 1996.

Mumford, Lewis. The Pentagon of Power. New York: Harcourt Brace Jovanovich, 1970.

Murray, Charles. Losing Ground: American Social Policy 1950-1980. New York: Basic Books, 1984.

Potter, Peter, ed. All About Death. New Canaan, Conn.: William Mulvey Inc., 1988.

Queens, Stuart A. and Robert W. Habenstein. The Family in Various Cultures. 3rd ed. Philadelphia: J. B. Lippincott, 1967.

Redhead, John A. Putting Your Faith to Work. New York. Abingdon Press, 1959.

Ries, A. and J. Trout. Positioning: The Battle for Your Mind. New York: McGraw-Hill, 1981.

Rogers, E. M., and F. Floyd Shoemaker. Communication of Innovations: A Cross Cultural Approach. 2nd ed. New York: Free Press, 1971.

Salmon, J.H.M. The French Religious Wars in English Thought. Oxford: Clarendon Press, 1959.

Sawyer, Avery F. Alternatives to the Decline and Fall of the United States: Toward a Broader Perception of Demographic Trends. Chicago. Bunbury Hall Publishers, 2000.

Scalia, Antonin. A Matter of Interpretation: Federal Courts and the Law. Princeton University Press, 1997.

Schroeder, John Frederick, ed. Maxims of Washington. Mount Vernon, Va.: Mount Vernon Ladies Association, 1942.

Seneca, Lucius Annaeus. Letters from a Stoic: Epistulae Morales Ad Lucilium. (The Penguin Classics 6210).

Sheehy, Gail. New Passages. New York: Random House, 1995.

Shield, Maurice. Congress, Contingency and Morality. Glen Oaks, Il.: Sandenhauser Free Press, 2001.

— Public Virtue and Private Vice. Glen Oaks, Il.: Sandenhauser Free Press, 1999.

Spong, John Shelby. Rescuing the Bible from Fundamentalism. San Francisco: Harper San Francisco, 1991.

Sumner, William Graham. What Classes Owe to Each Other: New York: Harper & Bros., 1883.

Tomlinson, Gerald, ed. and comp. Treasury of Religious Quotations. Englewood Cliffs, New Jersey: Prentice Hall, 1991.

Welter, Barbara. "The Cult of True Womanhood: 1820-1860." American Quarterly, XVIII (Summer 1966), pp. 162 ff.

Wright, David McCord. Democracy and Progress. New York: The Macmillan Co., 1949.

Wulff, Kimberly, ed. Epistemology and Temporality: From Catiline to Jimmy Carter. 5th ed. New Haven: The Seneca Press, 2000.

Zeltzer, Dr. Leonardo M. and Helena R. Zeltzer. Cemeteries of the Rich and Famous. New York: The Finale Press, 2006.

Zeltzer, Dr. Leonardo M. and Samantha Zeltzer. Mourning Secrets of the Stars. New York: The Finale Press., 2010.

Zeltzer, Samantha. The Magic of Mourning. New York: The Finale Press, 2011.

www.ingramcontent.com/pod-product-compliance
Lightning Source LLC
Chambersburg PA
CBHW071524040426
42452CB00008B/873